[trade SECRETS]
FOOD
AND
DRINK

trade SECRETS
FOOD AND DRINK

Alexandra Fraser

ORION

*With grateful thanks to the best
kept 'trade secrets': Jennie Sandford,
Paul Woolf and Lucy Vernall.*

First published in 1999 by Orion
An imprint of Orion Books Ltd
Orion House
5 Upper St Martin's Lane
London WC2H 9EA

Copyright © Maverick TV Ltd 1999

Maverick TV has asserted its rights
to be identified as the author of this work

All rights reserved. No part of this publication
may be reproduced, stored in a retrieval system,
or transmitted, in any form or by any means,
electronic, mechanical, photocopying, recording
or otherwise, without the prior permission
of the copyright holder.

A CIP catalogue record for this book
is available from the British Library

ISBN 0-75281-826-0

Printed in Great Britain by
Clays Ltd, St Ives plc

Contents

Foreword VII

1. Soups and Sauces 1
2. Eggs and Dairy 13
3. Meat and Fish 23
4. Fruit and Vegetables 49
5. Healthy Options 85
6. Entertaining 105
7. Feeding Children 121
8. Tools of the Trade 147
9. Baking and Sweets 171
10. Wine, Spirits and Beer 203
11. Saving the Day 221

Index 235

Foreword

'You are what you eat' makes complete sense. Surely if we fill our bellies with sun-ripened fruits, vitamin-packed vegetables and delicious home cooking we will radiate beauty and vitality.

Unfortunately, any good I might derive from consuming such delicious fare seems to be completely undone by the sheer effort of buying it, carrying it, preparing it, cooking it and serving it. Not to mention the entirely odious task of clearing up all the mess afterwards. Cookery books crammed with enticing glossy photos of enviable entrées, sumptuous salads and perfect puddings never seem to show the culinary carnage that ensues.

Nor, it seems to me, do these books tell the poor reader what to do when things go wrong. What *do* you do when your hollandaise sauce curdles, your soufflé resolutely refuses to rise and even the wine you might have drowned your sorrows in has bits of cork floating in it?

Panic not. We have persuaded professional chefs, restaurateurs, publicans and experts from across the food industry to let us in on their secrets. From our privileged access to their kitchens and cellars we have gathered together all the ingredients you will need to cater for every eventuality.

SOUPS AND SAUCES

'Beautiful soup, so rich and green,
Waiting in a hot tureen!
Who for such dainties would not stoop
Soup of the evening, beautiful soup!'
Alice's Adventures in Wonderland, Lewis Caroll

Soups

'I live on good soups, not on fine words.'
Jean-Baptiste Molière

To thicken stews and soups,
don't use flour – porridge oats are just as effective and much tastier too.

To give your soup a beautiful golden colour,
add some of an onion's outer skin. Remember to remove it from the soup before serving.

To give all soups a rich flavour and colour,
add a tablespoon of prune juice.

When making soup,
put a crustless piece of bread in the blender with the other ingredients to give the soup a lovely texture.

To thicken home-made soup quickly,
> just add some instant mashed potato before serving.

To get rid of congealed fat in a soup or stew,
> drop in an ice cube. It should attract the excess grease to it, gathering it in one place for you to remove.

If you like adding yoghurt to soups
> and casseroles but find that it separates, mix with a few tablespoonfuls of cooling stock before hand.

Remember, when you're making a purée to decorate soup,
> make sure it's the same consistency as the soup – if it's heavier it will just sink to the bottom.

If you've got room in your fridge,
> save the water that you have boiled potatoes in and use it for making soups. It's more nutritious than plain water and adds flavour and body to your cooking. Potato water will keep in a fridge for three or four days.

Reserve the liquid used
to soak dried mushrooms and freeze it. It will be a real boost to soups and sauces in the future.

Jazz up plain tinned soup
by stirring in some sherry or port.

Pep up boring bean or vegetable soup
with a large tablespoonful of balsamic vinegar.

A dash of lemon juice added to cream of mushroom soup
just before serving will cut through the richness of the soup and bring out the full flavour.

Draw a slice of bread across the top of soups or stews
to soak up excess grease.

Sauces

'The difference between good cookery and bad cookery can scarcely be more strikingly shown than in the manner in which sauces are prepared and served.'
Modern Cookery for Private Families,
1845, Eliza Acton

To avoid lumpy white sauce,
heat the milk before you add it.

If you have some gravy left over,
pour it into a small margarine tub, freeze it and keep it for stock.

For handy ready-made portions of apple sauce,
freeze large quantities of stewed apples in an ice-cube tray. Defrost some when you need them.

Instead of using plain water as a base
for gravies and sauces, save the water from boiling vegetables. It has more flavour, more goodness and it saves water.

To make mayonnaise more interesting,
add a pinch of curry powder or even some brown sauce.

To get the best from vinaigrette,
make it at least an hour before dressing the salad to allow time for the flavours to mix together.

To dress a salad evenly,
pour the dressing down the sides of the bowl rather than directly on to the salad.

Also,
try putting your dressing in a spray bottle to coat salad lightly. This can cut down on calories too!

Do your sauces stick to the spoon when serving them?

Dip the spoon in cold water or cold milk (if a milk-based sauce) and the sauce will run off it more easily.

To get the best from wine in sauces

– put the wine in a pan and bring it to the boil beforehand. Then set light to it with a match. The flame will burn off the alcohol and any sharpness. Add a touch of sugar to sweeten and add to the recipe.

Put too much salt in your sauce?

Dip a sugar cube into the sauce and swirl around on the surface for a minute or two.

Left-over wine?

Pour into ice-cub trays and freeze. The cubes are ideal for sauces, soups and stews.

Make your own chutney.
>Simply empty a packet of dates into a clean jam jar, cover with your favourite flavoured vinegar and leave for at least a week. It's cheap and delicious.

For a fresh-tasting home-made salad dressing,
>mix a pinch of paprika and a squeeze of lemon juice into a carton of plain yoghurt.

To get really rich curry sauces,
>add a little sugar to the butter or ghee while melting it.

To thicken gravy,
>add instant mashed potato.

Create your own flavoured vinegars, oils and mustards
>using your favourite herbs and spices – place the herbs or spices into the bottles or jars of vinegar and seal for at least a week.

Save left-over red wine in a screw-top bottle
and keep for sauces and salad dressings.

Left-over chicken, beef bones or vegetables?
Don't throw them out. If you've got room in your freezer put the whole lot in a sealed bag and freeze. You'll have all the ingredients to make a stock when required.

If you're making a tomato sauce
but the tomatoes are a little tart, try adding finely diced carrots at the start of cooking. They'll mellow the flavour.

Thicken spicy sauces
with unsweetened cocoa powder.

A spoonful of cream added to a sauce made with milk
will give the impression that it's made entirely with cream.

For no-fuss marinating,
pop the marinade and the meat into a self-seal bag. It takes up less room in the fridge than a bowl or plate and just needs a turn from time to time.

Remember
cold water brings out flavour and hot water seals flavour in. Always start a stock with cold water.

Try adding mustard or marmite to your gravy mixture
for a special gravy that packs a punch.

For a yummy sandwich filling,
mix honey and mayonnaise.

EGGS AND DAIRY

'See this egg. It is with this that one overturns all the schools of theology and all the temples on earth.'
Denis Diderot

Eggs

You can't make an omelette without breaking eggs.
Proverb

Don't waste energy boiling eggs continuously
– once the water's come to the boil, turn off the heat and leave the eggs in the pan for about 15 minutes.

To test whether an egg is properly hard boiled,
try spinning it on a hard surface. If it doesn't spin easily, it isn't quite cooked.

If you get a little bit of yolk in the white
when separating eggs, take a bit of tightly rolled kitchen towel that you have heated up in some boiling water and hold it near to the yolk. The heat will draw the yolk towards the towel.

Scramble eggs in a heat-proof glass bowl
   placed in a pan of boiling water. This way, you won't have to scrub an eggy saucepan afterwards.

Eggs will stay fresher
   for longer if stored pointed end down.

To stop boiling eggs cracking,
   add a cold metal spoon to the water before it comes to the boil.

For really fluffy omelettes,
   add a squirt of soda water to the egg mixture before cooking.

If you have trouble peeling hard-boiled eggs,
   crack the shells and soak them in cold water for a minute – the shells will slip off beautifully.

Eggs will whip more easily
   if left in cold water for ten minutes before breaking.

For perfect poached eggs

without a poacher, add white wine vinegar to the water, bring to the boil, crack in the eggs and reduce to simmer.

You can freeze egg whites

but not egg yolks.

To open raw quails' eggs

– take a small knife. Towards the flat end of the egg, gently push the blade of the knife into the shell. Turn the egg, keeping the knife in place, taking a circle of shell from the top of the egg. Then, carefully pour out the egg.

Here's a cracking tip for hard-boiling eggs

– boil ten or 15 eggs at one time. While boiling, add food colouring to the water. The shells of the cooked eggs will take on the colour of the dye. You can then look in the fridge and tell at a glance which eggs are hard-boiled and which are raw.

For extra fluffy scrambled eggs or omelettes,
 pour all the ingredients into a large plastic milk container and give it a good shake.

To separate lots of eggs at the same time,
 gently break them all into a bowl and with clean, careful hands scoop out the yolks – it's great fun!

Dairy

'Honest bread is all very well – it's the butter that makes the temptation.'
The Catspaw, Douglas William Jerrold

To keep cheese fresh for longer,
 wrap it in a cloth that you have dampened with distilled white vinegar.

Also, a sugar cube in the cheese box
 will extend the life of your cheeses.

Keep unopened cartons of double cream
fresher for longer by turning the carton upside down in the fridge.

To make really light whipped cream,
add a dash of ice-cold water just before the final whip.

For an instant and healthy milk shake,
whisk half yoghurt with half milk.

Make a truly de luxe creamy porridge
by stirring in a scoop of quality vanilla ice-cream during cooking.

Stop the sides of cheddar cheese going hard and waxy,
by spreading a thin layer of butter over the sides before you wrap the cheese up and put it away for the night.

Don't worry about keeping milk fresh
while you're camping, just mix muesli with milk powder, store in a sealable box until needed and add water as required.

Gently toast sliced or grated Parmesan cheese
under a low grill before serving it for
a better taste.

If a recipe calls for milk,
for a change – try yoghurt instead.

If a recipe calls for buttermilk
and you haven't got any, use ¼ cup milk
and ¾ cup yoghurt instead of one cup of
buttermilk.

To make delicious, creamy scrambled eggs,
beat in a tablespoon of mayonnaise for
every two eggs.

To prevent blocks of cheese going mouldy
before you have the chance to use them,
grate the cheese and store in a sealed
container in the fridge.

If you need softened butter
but have forgotten to take it out of the
fridge, try grating it on to a warm dish.

To test whether an egg is fresh or not,

hold it up to a burning candle. If there are black spots visible, the egg is bad.

To make better cheese on toast,

take the cheese out of the fridge 30 minutes before melting it. Cheese melts better and will not separate if it starts off at room temperature.

Fancy some de luxe cheese on toast?

Mix grated cheese with an egg for a scrummy bubbly topping. A pinch of chilli powder will give the mixture a bit of bite or try some chopped spring onion for a delicious extra flavour.

Store milk on fridge shelves,

not in the door as this usually isn't cold enough.

You can freeze milk for up to three weeks

without doing too much harm to it nutritionally. Skimmed freezes better than whole-fat milk. If you're off on holiday leave a carton in the freezer so you can make a cup of tea when you get back. Always thaw milk in the fridge and beat it if it separates.

If your little ones aren't keen on milk,
add it to food in place of water – they'll get all the goodness without realizing.

Whipping cream calls for cool temperatures
– refrigerate your utensils before you start.

MEAT AND FISH

'It is useless for the sheep to pass resolutions in favour of vegetarianism while the wolf remains of a different opinion.'
William Ralph Inge

Meat

> *'Upon what meat does this our Caesar feed*
> *That he is grown so great!'*
> *Julius Caesar*, William Shakespeare

To make cocktail sausages,
don't bother to buy the expensive ones in the shops. Just warm your hands and pinch and twist a chipolata in the middle so it forms two small cocktail sausages.

To make cracking pork crackling,
rub the fat with vinegar and then sprinkle on some salt. The acidity will make the crackling. Pigs are much leaner nowadays so it's more difficult to get good crackling.

Score pork with a Stanley knife
before putting it into the oven.

Gammon can be too salty;
>when boiling a ham, put some lemon juice on it to reduce the saltiness. This also keeps the meat nice and pink.

Don't bother to pluck a pheasant...
>skin it instead. The skin comes off like a sock!

If you get blood on a sheepskin coat,
>sprinkle potting compost on it and leave overnight. It works like blotting paper. Just brush it off in the morning.

Before plucking a chicken,
>soak the bird in boiling water for a minute or two and the feathers will come out more easily.

If sliced ham or tongue has dried out,
>soak it in a little milk for five minutes which will restore its flavour and texture.

Lots of people marinate
– but not for long enough. Marinades only work if left for at least 24 hours.

If you're cooking a big casserole,
put a sheet of tin foil between the pot and the lid to save having to wash up the grimy lid afterwards.

Does the meat seem a bit tough?
Squirt a little lemon juice into it before carving.

To ensure that the meat is tender,
always carve across the grain.

To serve really thin slices of cold meat,
place the joint in the freezer for half an hour before carving – even wafer-thin slices won't be a problem.

As an alternative to honey-roast ham,
try emptying a can of fizzy cola into the baking tray for really sweet-tasting meat.

To stop your gammon from curling

over when frying, simply make small snips roughly an inch apart around the edges with a pair of scissors.

Tenderize meat

by marinating it in distilled vinegar overnight.

If you've overdone the chilli in your meat curry,

squeeze the juice of half a lemon into the pot. Stir the half lemon into the curry for a few minutes before removing. All the chilli taste will have disappeared.

To rescue a casserole that has been over-salted,

just add fizzy water.

Alternatively,

place a raw, peeled potato in the casserole for ten minutes and then remove.

If there's too much fat on the top of your casserole

or sauce, gently float a piece of kitchen paper across the top and it will soak up the excess.

When grilling lots of sausages,

thread them onto skewers so that it's easier to keep turning them.

Your bacon will be really crispy

if you trim the rind with pinking shears before cooking it.

If you need to reduce fat,

but love the taste of bacon, try using turkey rashers as a substitute – they're virtually fat free.

For a low-fat gravy,

try separating the meat juices and fat by pouring them into a jug and adding ice cubes. The ice will cool down the gravy quickly, allowing you to spoon off the fat straight away.

Make your own marinade for pork;
> use a tablespoon of honey mixed with a teaspooon of grated ginger – sweet and spicy.

For a more subtle flavour in chilli con carne,
> use lemon or lime rind grated into the mix.

Try placing a layer of cream crackers
> or Pringles between the meat and the potato in a shepherd's pie or cottage pie – they'll absorb the juices from the sauce and keep the mashed potato fluffy.

To tenderize meat,
> cover it with slices of kiwi fruit for about 15 minutes and remove before cooking.

At Christmas,
> baste your turkey with fruit juice for that extra bit of taste.

To roast a turkey evenly,
begin roasting it upside down and only turn it right side up after about 45 minutes.

To add a bit more flavour to the turkey,
lift up the skin and rub olive oil and herbs onto the meat before cooking.

To stop a turkey sticking
to tin foil during cooking, place a piece of celery along the breast bone.

To skim the grease off stock
during cooking, drop in a cold lettuce leaf for ten seconds. The grease in the hot stock will stick to the lettuce and can be easily removed.

If you have left-over turkey,
take the stuffing out before putting the bird in the fridge, and refrigerate the stuffing in a separate bowl. You risk bacteria growing if you leave the stuffing inside.

To tenderize the meat in stews,
> add three or four wine corks to the pot. The corks release chemicals that both tenderize the meat and reduce cooking time. Remove them before serving!

To make top-quality meat gravy,
> wait until the fat has solidified and then remove it from the liquid.

To get the skin off chicken more easily,
> dip your hands in flour before you start, making it much less slippery.

To make sure the whole burger
> gets properly cooked, poke holes in the centre before putting it on the grill.

Keep poultry moist
> while roasting by placing a bowl of water in the bottom of the oven. Make sure you use a heat-proof bowl or roasting tin.

Before opening a packet of bacon,
> roll it up. It will make it easier to separate the slices.

To tenderize tough cuts of meat,

rub both sides with a mixture of vinegar, olive oil and perhaps a little salt. Then, put the meat in the fridge for two or three hours before cooking.

Freeze meat

in the coldest part of the freezer.

Save time struggling to get corned beef out of the can.

Pour hot water over the unopened can for a few minutes and the meat will slide out easily.

A turkey is only as good as the food that it eats

so try to find free-range birds that have been fed on a variety of grains.

Roasting a chicken?

Put some vegetables in a Pyrex bowl, cover with cold water and cook in the oven at the same time, and for as long as, the chicken to save using an additional ring on the cooker.

Mince or finely chop left-over meat
> from your Sunday roast to make cottage pie on Monday.

To speed up the cooking time of a boneless breast of chicken,
> place between pieces of waxed paper and flatten with a meat mallet. It will cook quickly and more evenly.

Fish

Fish and guests smell in three days.
Proverb

To ensure that you get the best range and quality of fish,
> choose a fishmonger that supplies local restaurants.

The most important thing when buying fish
is to ensure that it's really fresh.

Fresh fish should have a firm texture;
push your fingers into the flesh. If your indentation stays there, it's not really fresh.

Also, to tell if a fish is fresh,
check the brightness of the scales and the pinkness of the gills. The eyes must be clear, bright and never sunken.

Fresh sea fish
should be bright and not noticeably dry.

Fresh trout
should be slightly slimy to the touch.

The tail of a truly fresh fish
will be stiff.

When buying white fish fillets,
> look for neat trim fillets and a white translucent appearance.

Smoked fish
> should have a fresh smoky aroma and a really glossy appearance.

Frozen fish
> should be frozen hard with no signs of partial thawing and the packaging should be undamaged.

Don't buy plaice that has roe in it
> because it will be absolutely tasteless.

To tell if a salmon is fresh or farmed,
> hold the tail between your thumb and forefinger. Farmed fish have far less scales and are therefore more slippery. So if it slips through your fingers, you'll know it's been farmed.

Fresh fish should be used as soon as possible.
> However, it can be stored in the fridge overnight.

Keep fish cool.
Remove from the packaging and rinse in ice-cold water. Pat dry, cover and store near the bottom of the fridge.

Store fresh fish and smoked fish separately
so the flavours don't get mixed up.

Store cooked, ready-to-eat fish
(such as smoked mackerel, prawns and crab) separately from raw fish.

Before freezing your fish,
rinse it in water to create a protective ice glaze around the fish when it's frozen.

Soak fish like shark,
ray and skate in salt water for 20 minutes before cooking to remove the smell of ammonia.

Choose mussels with undamaged shells.

When cooking mussels,

make sure that all those that should open do so, by stirring them regularly in the saucepan. Sometimes mussels are prevented from opening by the sheer number in the pan.

Crab and lobster

should feel heavier than you would expect. This means that they will be meaty and juicy. If you are choosing from several, choose the ones that seem to feel too heavy for their size.

To store lobster,

soak some sheets of newspapers in cold water. Roll up the lobster in the newspaper and put in the fridge. The lobster will keep fresh for up to two days.

When preparing fish,

always use a razor-sharp knife.

Before filleting and skinning fish,

dip your fingers in salt. You'll get a much better grip.

Cut the fish from the bottom to the neck
and then chop off the head. The innards will pull out easily.

Scrape out the guts,
especially of larger fish, using a spoon.

When filleting a plaice,
start with the white side first. The head is on this side; it's quite knobbly so it's easier to grip.

To remove the bones from raw fish,
use a vegetable peeler. Run the peeler along the flesh, catching bones in the centre slit. Twist the peeler and pull the bones out.

Remove fiddly bones
from salmon fillets with tweezers.

In salmon and trout,

there is a line along the spine of the fish (a black kidney shape in a trout and a red blood patch in a salmon) which doesn't taste very nice. You can remove it easily by running your fingernail along the spine.

The head-end third of cod

contains all the large noticeable bones. Run your thumb along the top of the fish. Where the bumps stop marks the end of these bones (tail-end of cod only has small bones). If you cut a V-shape in the back of the fish up to where the bumps end, you will have a boneless piece of fish.

When preparing monkfish,

cut the head off and pull the skin off from the tail towards the head. Then remove the membrane that covers the flesh of the fish before cooking, otherwise the fish will have a chewy texture.

To clear fish guts and scales from your chopping board,
>   use a clean window squeegee.

Ideally, clean fish on newspaper,
>   this keeps your board clean and means you can wrap the smelly waste up and put it straight into the bin.

Mustard removes fishy smells
>   from wooden boards.

Alternatively,
>   clean wooden chopping boards with half a lemon dipped in salt. This also prevents the surface from staining.

To remove strong food smells from plastic chopping boards,
>   give them a rub down with a cut lemon.

Always dry wooden chopping boards
>   upright and not flat to stop them from warping.

Prevent that lingering fish smell on plates
> by putting a tablespoon of malt vinegar in the washing-up water.

To clean a pan after cooking
> and thoroughly remove the fishy smell, leave some cold tea in the pan for ten minutes before you come to wash it.

To remove a fishy smell from your hands,
> rinse them in lemon juice.

To reduce the unpleasant fishy smell
> when poaching fish, add some celery leaves to the pot.

Always pick a hake up by its eyes
> so you don't cut your hands.

Crab should be placed alive in cold water
> and put on a low heat. If you place it in hot water, its membrane will let water in and its bits will fall off! Heat it up slowly to make sure your presentation is perfect.

When crab has been cooked,
> take the shell off and remove the 'dead man's fingers'; these are the gills and taste really nasty. There are five on either side of the inner body; make sure you get them all out.

Don't crush crab and lobster claws;
> use the handle of a teaspoon to gently get the meat out instead.

A clean and easy way to coat fish in batter
> or breadcrumbs is to place the fish in a freezer bag with the batter or crumbs and shake gently until it is covered. This ensures an even coating without any really thick clumps.

Before shallow-frying fish,
> first dip it into well-seasoned flour. This will create a protective layer which helps to form a good crust and keep the fish moist.

Always mix the pre-mixed batter

from supermarkets with chilled water. If the water is too warm, the batter will ferment. Then drop the batter-covered fish into really hot fat. If your fat isn't hot enough, the fish will just absorb the fat and the batter won't be crispy. Very hot fat instantly seals the batter.

Whisk your batter

for as long as possible – the more you whisk, the lighter and fluffier the batter will be.

To make an unusual and delicious batter

for deep-fried fish replace the milk in the batter recipe with the same quantity of beer. Allow the batter to stand in the fridge for half an hour before using. The starch grains in the flour absorb the gassy beer, producing a lighter mixture.

To make batter stick properly

to fish or whatever else you're battering, add ½ teaspoon of sugar per ½ pint of batter.

To keep fried fish warm,
> don't stack it or cover it up – this will make it soggy.

To stop fish from falling apart
> after it's been fried, dip it in boiling water before you fry it.

To test if fish is cooked,
> look for flesh which is opaque and feels firm to the touch. You should be able to insert a knife easily and peel the skin away.

Fish can be cooked straight from the freezer
> – just add a couple of extra minutes to the cooking time.

Pieces of bacon laid over skinned white fish fillets
> will keep them moist while cooking.

Cook fish in foil parcels
> in the oven to give delicious, moist morsels.

You don't need an expensive steamer for fish

just put a colander over a pan of boiling water and cover the colander with a large lid.

If grilling a whole fish

(mackerel, for example), slash the skin three or four times on the diagonal on both sides. This prevents the skin from breaking open when cooked.

Skinning a fish is fiddly.

Flash grill the fish first under a very hot grill and the crispy, scorched skin will lift off effortlessly.

Fish cooks quickly

and the golden rule is never to overcook it.

To cook delicious juicy fish,

wrap it in cling film and place in boiling water so that none of the natural flavours escape.

To prevent fish skin from sticking to the frying pan,
>rub the fish with salt, leave for 15 minutes, rinse and rub dry. Then cook.

For a tasty, crunchy coating for fish
>or potato croquettes, first dip the fish or potato in egg and then roll in crushed crisps – just choose your favourite flavour.

It's easy to cook trout in the microwave
>– try brushing each side with some balsamic vinegar for a lovely flavour.

To slice tuna thinly,
>pop it in the freezer for an hour before use to make the task easier.

To stop fish going soggy during cooking,
>sprinkle it with salt and leave for half an hour before cooking.

To make haddock less salty,
>poach it in milk.

To make opening sardine tins easy, don't even try to use the troublesome key, just turn the tin upside down and use a tin opener.

FRUIT AND VEGETABLES

'Good mashed potato is one of the great luxuries of life.'
Lindsay Bareham

Fruit

*'What wond'rous life is this I lead
Ripe apples drop about my head
The nectarine and curious peach
Into my hands themselves do reach.'*
The Garden, Andrew Marshall

APPLES

An apple a day keeps the doctor away.
Proverb

To find out if a Cox's apple is ready to eat,
shake it. If the pips rattle, it's perfect!

When buying Golden Delicious apples,
looks can be deceiving. Choose the ones with more brown spots on the skin. The more spots, the more flavour.

To peel apples in half the time,
blanche them first in boiling water.

Make great teethers
for babies using dried apple rings.

Stop cut apples from going brown
– sprinkle them with lemon juice.

Don't lose all the filling when cooking baked apples
– before you put them in the oven, plug the hole with a little piece of marzipan.

If your cooked apples taste bland,
grate some orange or lemon peel over the top and bake for a further ten minutes.

To ensure apples remain crisp
and juicy store them in perforated plastic bags in the salad crisper of your fridge.

To stop fruit in a bowl from going mouldy,
place a piece of kitchen roll in the bottom of the dish to absorb all the moisture.

CITRUS FRUIT

'Oranges and Lemons say the bells of St Clements.'
Traditional Nursery Rhyme

To freeze fruit
line the trays with the waxed paper from the inside of cereal packets.

To get the most juice out of a lemon,
cut it in half and warm both halves in the oven for a few minutes before use.

When choosing lemons and oranges,
always go for the fruit that seems to feel too heavy for its size.

If you need to keep lemons fresh
for a long time, store them covered in cold water.

Old, wrinkly lemons
can be restored to their former glory by boiling them in water for a few minutes then leaving them to cool.

If your lemons are over ripe,
cut them in half and soak them in hot water then use them to clean your windows.

Before you grate citrus fruit,
rinse the grater in ice-cold water. After use, the peel will come away from it much more easily.

Citrus peel
helps to get a barbecue going, and makes it smell great.

Oranges and grapefruits look much prettier
in fruit salad if you can remove the white pith. To make the task easy, soak the fruit in boiling water for about five minutes before you peel off the skin and the pith should come away at the same time.

Dry orange peel
    in the Aga or oven to make firelighters.

If you suffer from constipation,
    a couple of drops of linseed oil in some orange juice will help get things moving.

To get the juice out of a citrus fruit more easily,
    roll the fruit back and forth over a hard surface before cutting it in half.

When you have squeezed an orange or lemon,
    remove the rind and store it in a jar or in the freezer. Use the rind to flavour salads, stews and cakes.

The smoother a lemon skin is,
    the juicier the lemon is.

To save money on lemons
    buy lots when they're on special offer. Squeeze the juice out and freeze it in ice-cube trays. When a recipe calls for lemon juice, just take out the required number of lemon ice cubes and add to the pot.

To get just a few drops of juice out of a lemon
without wasting the whole thing... prick
the lemon with a toothpick. Squeeze out
the few drops that you need. Stick the
toothpick back into the hole and put
the lemon in the fridge.

BANANAS

*'But the fruit that can fall without shaking
indeed is too mellow for me.'*
Lady Montagu

Bananas gone brown?
Don't fancy eating them? Use them to
make delicious banana bread.

An alternative use for brown bananas
is in banana milkshakes where you don't
see that they've gone brown.

Ripen green bananas
by leaving a red tomato next to them.

To stop bananas from turning black
in a fruit salad, leave the unpeeled fruit covered in cold water for 10 or 15 minutes before peeling.

Banana trees for hanging bananas
on are great because bananas kept in the fruit bowl make the other fruit go off. But what happens when you're down to your last banana? Make sure that the last one has a long stem and then poke the banana tree's hook through the stem.

OTHER FRUITS

'The heaventree of stars hung with humid nightblue fruit.'
Ulysses, James Joyce

Bounce your cranberries
to find out if they are fresh or not. If they bounce, they are!

To trim gooseberries,
use baby nail clippers.

For a fruit salad

with a difference, use lemonade instead of fruit juice. For a special celebration, try Champagne instead.

To chop dried fruit

wet the blade of the knife so the fruit doesn't stick to it.

Rhubarb

is a great blood purifier.

Don't always buy with your eyes

– the more crinkly the skin on a honeydew melon, the sweeter it will be inside.

If rhubarb is too acidic

for you try leaving it to soak in cold black tea for an hour before using.

Alternatively

before cooking, chop the rhubarb into 2-in/5-cm pieces. Dissolve one heaped teaspoon of bicarbonate of soda per pint of cold water and soak the fruit in it.

Liquidize watermelon
for just a few seconds for a refreshing drink. You don't even need to pick out the seeds because they'll sink to the bottom.

To bring out the flavour of strawberries
when cooking them in desserts, add a touch of balsamic vinegar to the recipe.

To pep up pineapple chunks,
sprinkle with black pepper.

Pineapple juice
helps ease a sore throat.

When you buy or pick a quantity of berries,
there are often small twigs or leaves mixed in with them. The quickest way to get rid of the twigs and leaves without harming the fruit is to pour them from one container to another across the path of a fan.

To keep strawberries fresh
in the fridge for as long as a week, wash and dry them (but don't remove the green stalks) and put them in a sealed glass jar.

Keep fruit and veg for longer
by storing it in paper bags rather than plastic.

To check if a bunch of grapes is fresh,
shake the bunch gently. If any grapes fall off, they are not fresh.

For a tasty bolognaise sauce,
try adding raisins, sliced apricots and apples to the mince.

Chopped fruit often goes brown.
It's a good idea to keep some bottled lemon juice in a spray bottle in the fridge. Whenever you chop fruit just give it a quick squirt of lemon and that should stop it browning.

Test to see if a pineapple is ripe.
   You should be able to pull a leaf from the top easily.

To tell if a shelled nut is fresh or not,
   shake it. If it rattles, it's not fresh.

For a nutty addition to dishes,
   use sesame seeds that have been toasted until brown.

Vegetables

'I do not like broccoli and I haven't liked it since I was a little kid. I am the President of the United States and I am not going to eat any more.'
George Bush

For whiter than white cauliflower,
    add some milk to the water when cooking it.

Carrots are easier to scrape
    if dunked in boiling water first.

Mushrooms won't shrink
    when cooked if you soak them in a little boiling water first.

To cook delicious broad beans,
    add some chopped parsley to the water.

If a recipe calls for 'finely chopped onions'
just grate or blend some of them instead of chopping – it will save you time and tears!

To make onions brown more quickly when frying,
add a pinch of sugar. They'll also taste scrummy and slightly caramelized.

To absorb the smell of frying onions,
put a sheet of wet newspaper close to the hob.

If you want raw onions in your salad
but are worried that they will taste too strong, soak them in some tepid water first.

Has your lettuce has gone limp?
Pop it in a bowl with a piece of rinsed coal and leave for several minutes.

If you only need to use the tomatoes
>from the tin and not the juice, pour the left-over juice into an ice-cube tray for use in gravy at a later date.

Soggy tomatoes
>will firm up if soaked in salty water for ten minutes.

Prepare your potatoes the night before.
>To stop them becoming discoloured, leave them in a pan of water along with a small lump of coal. They will stay looking fresh until the next day.

If you're chopping an onion,
>place a small piece of bread under your top lip – you may feel silly but there'll be no more tears!

Store onions and garlic in the foot of some sheer tights
>and hang them up to keep them dry and fresh.

Peeling garlic can be fiddly.
>Peel down the stem of the clove and soak in boiling water for a few minutes. The skin will then come straight off.

To ripen tomatoes quickly,
>place them in a brown paper bag along with one ripe tomato.

Don't store tomatoes
>in a fridge because they will blister.

If you do have to keep your tomatoes in the fridge,
>take them out a couple of hours before eating, as they become juicier at room temperature.

Make your lettuce last longer
>by cutting out the core and sprinkling sugar into the cavity.

Tear lettuce instead of cutting it
>to avoid the leaves turning brown.

It doesn't have to end in tears.
> Store an onion in the fridge for several hours before using and you won't cry when you peel it.

The more wrinkled a red pepper is,
> the sweeter and riper the taste.

Store mushrooms in a paper bag
> to stop them sweating.

To keep watercress fresh for longer,
> immerse the leaves – but not the roots – in a jug of water.

Freshen up bad breath
> instantly by chewing two or three sprigs of watercress and a couple of grapes.

Keep water fresh;
> put a watercress leaf into a jug before filling it with water; this will keep the water fresh for longer.

Avocado pears make excellent face masks.
Just mash them up and smear them on for that perfect complexion.

Always buy broccoli with tight heads
– this way they won't drop off when you cook them.

Look out for really purple turnips
– the more purple the turnip, the better it will taste.

Aubergines
can be either male or female – both taste good.

To keep salad really fresh,
put a saucer upside down in the bottom of the bowl to collect any spare moisture.

Cabbage can stink
when it's being cooked. A bay leaf added to the boiling water will stop the smell without affecting the taste of the vegetable.

Tart up new potatoes or chips

with a couple of teaspoons of mint jelly over the top instead of butter or ketchup.

Make a quick chilli sauce using left-over vegetables.

Pop them in a pan with some whole chillies and stew them gently.

Boil carrots the healthy way

– leave them in their skins to keep the goodness in. The skins will scrape away easily afterwards if you plunge them into cold water.

To give cauliflower a bit more flavour

substitute chicken stock for plain water – alternatively just add a stock cube to the water.

If your roast potatoes take an age to brown,

sprinkle a little flour over them as they cook.

For perfect mash
> drop a teaspoon of sugar in with your boiling potatoes – it will make them more floury and they'll fluff up better.

Carrots will keep fresh
> in the fridge for weeks if you trim the tops and bottoms and put them in a plastic container.

To turn oven chips into a crispy and tasty treat,
> sprinkle them with sea salt during cooking.

For a delicious alternative topping for shepherd's pie,
> add cream cheese to the mashed potato.

You'll make chopping garlic easier,
> if you sprinkle a little salt on it first.

A good way to use left-over mashed potato
is to make savoury croquettes. Try adding finely chopped onion, tomato, parsley, even tuna and grated cheese. Mix well, form croquettes, roll in flour and fry.

Try putting salad dressing into a spray bottle
so that you can control the amount you use – there's nothing worse than soggy lettuce!

A cheap and easy alternative to using haricot beans
is to drain a tin of economy baked beans and rinse off the tomato sauce. Remember they're pre-cooked so adjust any recipe accordingly.

Use a balloon whisk to stir your rice,
you'll find it keeps the grains separated and fluffy.

If you can't get the last drops of salad cream
out of the bottle, add some mustard powder and a little vinegar – it makes a great salad dressing.

Peanut butter will spread easily
if you add half a teaspoon of sunflower oil to the jar and stir in well.

Take a bottle of capers,
drain off the vinegar and replace with olive oil. After a couple of weeks, the oil sweetens the taste.

Spice up your sex life with a carrot!
Carrots are full of beta carotene, which produces sex hormones.

Don't throw away left-over lentils
– fry them in a big pan with a splash of oil until dry. It makes a great topping for toast.

When cooking asparagus,
wedge the bundles upright in the pan using potatoes.

Don't throw away elderly garlic bulbs.
Plant them in a sunny spot, and water. The resulting garlic shoots are excellent in salad.

Keep a nettle patch.
Don't allow it to flower, but pick the nettle tops to use in cooking. The cooking gets rid of the sting and the taste is like spinach. For a tasty supper dish, boil new shoots for two to three minutes, drain and serve with butter.

Never buy artichokes
if they have brown patches.

To keep artichokes fresh
for a bit longer, cut off the dry ends and put the stems in a jar of water, adding a teaspoon of sugar to the water.

For a perfectly chopped onion,
skin it and put it on the chopping board root-end down. Cut downwards, but don't cut all the way through the onion. Turn the onion round and slice across the cuts.

Rose petals
 are edible and very tasty. They also look really pretty scattered across salads.

Here's the best way to skin tomatoes.
 Cut a shallow 'x' in the bottom of the tomato. Put it into rapidly boiling water until the skin starts to split. Immediately pop the tomato into a bowl of ice water and leave until cool. The skin should now peel off like magic.

To stop broccoli smelling while cooking,
 put a piece of red pepper in the pot with it while boiling.

To stop Brussels sprouts falling apart
 during boiling, cut an 'x' into the bottom of the sprout with a sharp knife before cooking.

Use vegetable broth rather than oil
 in a stir-fry to cut down on the fat.

To peel a garlic clove easily,
> press either side against the chopping board before peeling.

To remove the smell of onions from your hands
> after chopping, turn on the cold tap and rub your hands up and down the neck of the tap. This only works with stainless steel taps. If you don't have stainless steel taps, try rubbing your hands with a stainless steel spoon instead.

To stop onions making you cry,
> burn a candle nearby while chopping them.

To keep olive oil fresh
> – buy a large jar of olive oil but pour the oil into a number of smaller jars. Air affects the quality of the oil, so if you leave it in a large jar, as the amount

of oil decreases and the amount of air increases, the quality of the oil will diminish.

To prevent an unpleasant odour
when boiling cauliflower or cabbage, tear a slice of bread into small chunks and add it to the pot. The bread will absorb the smell. Rye bread works especially well.

When chopping up chilli peppers,
avoid getting hot stuff on your skin by coating your hands with vegetable oil before handling them.

To keep potatoes firm while boiling,
add vinegar to the water (one part vinegar to two parts water). Add a little salt too.

Be careful if wearing contact lenses
when chopping shallots or chillies, the smells have been known to permeate the lenses and harm the eyes.

To check the quality of raw beans,
put them in water. If they sink, they're good. If they float, throw them away.

If your string beans
have been around for a week and are starting to toughen, add some sugar to the water when cooking.

If your red cabbage turns blue
or purple while boiling, add a tablespoon of vinegar to the water and the cabbage will turn red again.

To get the best out of slightly old vegetables
while boiling, add salt to the boiling water to help retain flavour and colour.

Raw carrots taste best
if left in the fridge overnight in a pot of iced water. Add a little vinegar to the water first.

Left-over cucumber?
   Slice, sauté on both sides until
   brown and serve with cream cheese.
   Lovely!

To prevent potatoes sprouting
   before you have a chance to use
   them, put an apple in the same bag
   as the spuds.

To get baked beans out of the can,
   take the tin off the shelf and turn the
   can upside down, open as normal and
   you'll find all of the beans shoot out
   – simple but very effective.

Or, to make really sure that every single bean comes out –
   use a can-opener to remove the top,
   place a plate over the top and turn over
   quickly. Then, use the can opener on
   the other end, but don't throw away the
   circle of metal. Instead, push it through

the can at the same time as lifting the
can up. Take care you don't cut your
fingers.

To make the best of left-over veg,
keep a plastic container in the fridge.
Whenever you have left-over vegetables,
put them in the container and when the
container is full, make the contents into
a soup or stew.

To make peeling onions easier,
soak them in water for a few minutes
first.

To keep lettuce fresh for longer,
wrap it in a paper towel, put it a plastic
bag and keep it in the fridge.

For firm corn-on-the-cob,
add salt to the water while boiling.

To stop rice sticking
together, add a few drops of lemon juice to the water while boiling.

Celery keeps for longer
if wrapped in foil.

Don't throw out the dark, outside leaves from cauliflowers.
Remove the stalks and chop the leaves up finely. Add them to soups.

For an exciting spread for sandwiches,
freeze some olive oil in a plastic container. When the olive oil is cold and thick, spread it on.

Never store apples and carrots together
because the apples give off a gas that makes the carrots go bitter.

And, never store potatoes and onions together either.
>The potatoes will spoil faster.

To keep tomatoes for longer,
>store them with the stem down.

To get a subtle garlic taste in soup,
>before you start cooking, rub a cut garlic clove around the pan.

To stop potatoes falling apart while you boil them,
>turn the heat right down and simmer them for longer, rather than boiling them vigorously and cooking them too fast.

To make celery that bit crisper,
>put it in a bowl of iced water and leave it in the fridge for a few hours.

The brighter the colour of a dried bean,
>the fresher the bean.

For a subtle garlic flavour
spear a clove with a toothpick and dip it into the pan for 30 seconds every three minutes.

To preserve garlic after peeling,
place it in a jar and cover with olive oil. If you store it in the fridge, it will keep for up to four months.

The stronger broccoli smells,
the less fresh it is.

For crisp baked potato skins,
brush the potato with a little oil before cooking.

A good artichoke
will make a slight squeaking noise when handled.

Wrinkled green or yellow peppers aren't bad
– they just have a mellower flavour.

Buy potatoes that are of similar sizes
>   to avoid different cooking times.

For quick-cooking roast potatoes,
>   remove the centre lengthwise with an apple corer. For a sumptuous flavour, place rolled bacon strips in the hollow.

Singe the root end of your onions
>   – then they'll store for much longer.

Left-over Brussels sprouts
>   and potatoes from your Sunday roast make lovely bubble and squeak. Just fry all the left-overs up together.

Leave your bubble and squeak in the pan
>   to go nice and crispy before serving it. The crispy bits have more taste.

Boil up your cabbage with salt, pepper and butter
>   – the strained juice makes a great drink to aid digestion.

Keep cauliflower white
by adding two tablespoons of lemon juice or white wine vinegar to the cooking water.

Try cooking corn-on-the-cob
in equal parts of milk and water to tenderize the kernels.

Alternatively,
top with a couple of knobs of butter, a generous amount of pepper and wrap in tin foil. Roast in the oven for 20 to 30 minutes for a really intense flavour.

Freshly grated horse-radish
will pep up tired mashed potato.

If you find canned vegetables
taste tinny, drain them then blanch in boiling water for one minute and rinse in cool water.

Tight for time?
Chop a quantity of onions, green peppers and celery at the beginning of the week and refrigerate in individual well-sealed containers. Dip into them as required.

If you have half an avocado left over,
do not remove the stone. Store the avocado in the fridge – leaving the stone in will stop the flesh browning so quickly.

A lot of people don't like the taste of olives in brine.
Try putting them on to simmer in some fresh water for ten minutes. Drain well.

HEALTHY OPTIONS

'There was an old person of Dean
Who dined on one pea and one bean
For he said "more than that
  would make me too fat"
That cautious old person of Dean.'

One Hundred Nonsense Pictures and Rhymes,
Edward Lear

HEALTHY OPTIONS

Savoury

One should eat to live, not live to eat.
Proverb

You can have healthy roast potatoes!
 Parboil them, then place on a baking tray lined with parchment paper. Roast in the top half of the oven.

Mushrooms can be 'fried' in water,
 as a low-fat alternative to butter or oil.

Dried beans are full of goodness
 but also full of gas! To reduce their gassy effect always dispose of the soaking water and cook them in fresh water.

Also, if you are prone to wind,
 rinse tinned beans such as kidney and flageolet in fresh water before using. This will also reduce your salt intake.

To get the best results from Puy lentils
 just add a teaspoon of vinegar and a sugar cube to the cooking water.

If you want to lose weight from your hips,
avoid spicy foods because they over stimulate the glands that cause fat storage in your hips and bum.

For a healthy pastry base
that you can use in quiches and pizza, substitute wholemeal breadcrumbs mixed with plain low-fat yoghurt for plain flour.

If you're watching your fat intake
but crave take-away curry, buy it, leave it to cool and place in the fridge. When the ghee or fat solidifies skim it off – and hey presto, a low-fat curry that will taste delicious!

Eat vegetable soup
as a starter to lose weight. The fibre causes the rest of the meal to pass through your digestive system more quickly.

To reduce the amount you eat,
    turn out the lights. Dim lights make you want to eat less.

Also, to reduce the amount you eat,
    use smaller dishes. Large plates make you want to eat as much as you can fit on to them. It's all psychological.

Worried that you eat too quickly?
    Use chop-sticks!

Eat eggs to clear up a cold
    – they're high in zinc, which helps cure colds.

To get rid of a filthy cold, eat a strong curry
    – it will 'sweat' the cold out.

If cholesterol's a problem
    and you want to cut down on the number of eggs you eat, replace eggs in baking recipes with a tablespoon of soya flour mixed in with a tablespoon of water.

To persuade your kids to eat healthier cereal,
>mix half a portion of healthy stuff with half a helping of something less wholesome!

Here's a simple way to reduce calories
>and fat in your favourite pies. Don't cover the top with pastry – opt for a healthy open pie which is just as tasty.

Need a simple low-fat dip?
>Prick an aubergine all over and cook on high power in the microwave for ten minutes.

Spice up corn-on-the-cob
>with a squeeze of lime and a pinch of chilli powder for the delicious flavour of South America without the usual indulgence of butter.

For mashed potato
> without the butter, cream and milk, try beating in some of the hot cooking water. To make the spuds really light and fluffy you'll need lots of elbow grease but the exercise will help reduce those calories!

Alternatively,
> try using low-fat buttermilk or yoghurt.

For spuds that are high on flavour
> but low on calories try drizzling some balsamic vinegar over cooked potatoes.

To make thick broths
> without adding fat or flour just remove a portion of your soup from the pan, purée it and put it back in.

There's no need to fry French toast in oil or butter.
> Just pop it into a hot oven for ten minutes, turning once.

Try using minced turkey
> instead of beef in mince dishes like chilli or spaghetti bolognaise. It has less fat and calories and you can always 'beef' up the flavour using a beef stock cube.

To remove excess fat from soup
> and stock, fill a plastic bag with ice and drag it right across the surface. The fat will cling to the ice-cold bag.

Alternatively
> pour your stock through a large funnel filled with ice cubes.

To remove fat from tinned soup,
> place the can in the fridge. When it's cold, open the tin and scoop the separated fat off from the top.

When serving wine at a dinner party
> – always give everyone a glass of mineral water too. They'll quench their thirst with the water and sip the wine more slowly.

The simplest way to get a healthy diet
is to eat more fruit and vegetables. You should ideally eat five different portions a day – remember, 'eat five to stay alive!'

Don't add oil
to boiling pasta water as your sauce will slip off the pasta. A really good sauce should literally coat the pasta.

Raw spaghetti
makes an excellent firelighter.

To check if your pasta is cooked,
try flinging a piece against the oven door or the fridge. If it sticks, it's cooked.

Never rinse your pasta
– the starch helps the sauce stick to the pasta.

Children love pasta
– a bit of food colouring in the cooking water might make it even more fun!

Pasta bake
is cheap and easy, and an excellent way to use up left-overs. Simply pile any left-over vegetables in a dish with some cooked pasta. Add a tin of tomatoes or some baked beans, and cook.

Bored with rice?
Go for great presentation by packing it into small, shaped moulds (a small tea cup would do). Spraying the mould with a non-stick cooking spray makes this easier. Then turn it out like a jelly onto the plate.

Remember rice triples its volume
when cooked so be sure to use a big enough pan.

Always fluff cooked rice with a fork,
this allows the steam to escape and stops the grains sticking together.

Cooked rice keeps well in the freezer
so make plenty and freeze the extra.

To make rice bright white,
> squeeze some lemon juice into the water while boiling.

Add toasted nuts to rice
> while boiling to enhance the nuttiness.

Sweet

'Tell me what you eat, and I will tell you what you are.'
Anthelme Brillat, Savarin

Love double cream, but trying to cut down on the calories?
> Evaporated skimmed milk makes an excellent substitute when slightly frozen.

Substitute dessicated coconut
> for some of the sugar when making a topping for fruit crumble.

For a healthy but tasty pudding,
>add some low-calorie drinking chocolate powder to natural yoghurt and some dried fruit such as sultanas, apricots, raisins. Leave overnight to allow the flavours to mingle.

A sugar-free way
>to enjoy a rhubarb tart is to add chopped dates instead.

Do you like fizzy drinks but worry about tooth decay?
>Use a straw – it reduces the contact between your teeth and the drink.

Trying to get used to sugar-free drinks?
>Put a little sugar around the rim of the glass – just enough to taste on the lips.

If you take a lot of medication,
>lay off the grapefruit juice. It can reduce the body's ability to absorb some drugs.

Plain, low-fat yoghurt
　　makes a healthier alternative to sour cream in recipes.

A frozen banana will stop hunger cravings
　　– its natural sweetness will give you energy without adding on extra pounds. Peel, wrap in cling film and freeze. It will take ages to eat as well!

Do you love ginger bread
　　but could do without the fat? Try replacing the fat in the recipe with pumpkin. It's tasty, low in calories and cholesterol, and is extremely good for you.

Frozen sheets of filo pastry
　　can be used as a low-fat alternative to shortcrust or puff.

Replace full-fat chocolate with cocoa powder
　　in cakes and desserts for a low-calorie treat.

Fancy a vitamin-packed light dessert to finish off a meal?
> Try making fruit granita using freshly squeezed grapefruit or orange juice. Add a splash of your favourite liqueur and poor into a shallow plastic container. Freeze the mixture, giving it the occasional gentle stir. You should get a pretty, crystal-like consistency.

Herbs and Spices

'Better is a dinner of herbs where love is than a stalled ox and hatred therewith.'
The Bible, Book of Proverbs

If you frequently use fresh herbs,
> save the measuring cups from medicine bottles. They can be used for measuring herbs and spices.

Make sure your parsley stays green,
> only add it to a sauce once the liquid has boiled.

Freeze parsley on its stem
in a clear plastic bag. When you need it, remove from the freezer and rub together. Your parsley is automatically chopped.

For garlic breath,
chew some parsley.

Keep flies away
– place fresh mint on the kitchen sill.

Add herbs to your barbecue
for even sweeter aromas.

Prevent car sickness
– chew some crystallized ginger.

If you smoke but want to kick the habit,
try chewing on liquorice root.

Ease painful indigestion
– drop cardamom pods into your coffee.

To get the best out of spices,
roast them before use.

To dry herbs instantly,
place them in the microwave for a few seconds. This works especially well with parsley.

To chop fresh herbs finely,
use a pizza cutter.

Try crumbling a vegetable stock cube
onto Welsh rarebit for a different taste.

Freeze herbs.
Chop them and pack into ice-cube trays, then cover with water before putting the tray into the freezer. When you defrost them, they'll taste as good as fresh.

Keep fresh herbs longer
– grind a handful in a food processor, add four tablespoons of vegetable oil and refrigerate.

When a recipe calls for the leaf of a fresh herb
to be added during cooking, add the stem of the herb instead. The stem has a stronger taste and, because it has less chlorophyll than the leaf, it won't add a green tint to the dish.

Mix dried herbs with fresh parsley
and no one will notice you've used dried herbs.

Save empty spice jars
– the re-fill packs are cheaper than buying replacement jars.

Pep up dried stuffing mix.
Use a dissolved vegetable stock cube instead of plain water.

To keep ground herbs fresh,
store them in a container that doesn't let in light.

Odds and ends of fresh root ginger
can be preserved in rice wine.

For garlic popcorn
>just add a peeled clove to the popping oil.

When a recipe calls for you to fry onions and garlic
>always add the garlic last to prevent burning.

If you don't have fresh herbs
>mix dried with lemon juice and a chopped onion and allow to stand for about 15 minutes.

Always bruise a bouquet garni slightly
>with a mallet or rolling pin to release the aromatic oils before placing in your pot.

For a home-made bouquet garni
>place bay leaves, thyme, parsley, cloves, allspice and black peppercorns onto a foil square. Fold and seal, and pierce with a pin to release flavours.

Alternatively if you have a tea ball,
>just pop the ingredients in and hang over the rim of your pan.

Chop mint the easy way
>– sprinkle some sugar on it first.

Freeze chopped chives in ice cubes for convenience
>– it saves fiddling about when you're in a hurry.

If you've been told to reduce your salt intake,
>try using dill seeds, crushed or ground, as a substitute.

Reduce the cooking smells from cabbage water;
>add a few caraway seeds to the pan.

Pop a bay leaf into stored flour
>to deter weevil.

Remember basil is one of the few herbs to increase its flavour when cooked,
> so always add at the end of cooking unless you want a really strong flavour.

Tear basil leaves rather than chopping them.

Sage is the ideal herb to use with meat
> as it aids digestion of fat and its antiseptic qualities help to kill off any bugs in the meat as it cooks.

ENTERTAINING

'Strange to see how a good dinner and feast reconciles everybody.'
Samuel Pepys

If your tablecloth is stained

and you've got guests arriving any minute, don't panic! Scatter some rose or flower petals onto the cloth for an effective and pretty solution.

If you are worried about damaging your table,

put some cling film across the wood before laying the table. If you are concerned about hot dishes burning the wood, put a blanket underneath the tablecloth.

Don't be a stranger to your guests.

The worst mistake people make is to throw a dinner party but spend all evening in the kitchen. Always choose menus that you can prepare in advance.

Provide contrast and variety

– go for different flavours and textures. Meat, followed by fish or the other way round. Don't have too many spicy tastes or rich flavours in one meal.

People usually try too hard when entertaining.
Stick to dishes you have made before, rather than launching into an ambitious recipe plucked out of a book! And don't try to put together a really exotic menu – if the main course is rich, try some sliced melon for starters. Likewise, if fancy puds are your thing, serve a simple main course of grilled fish or steak and salad.

Candles always add atmosphere to a meal.
Make sure yours are below eye level though so that your guests can see each other!

To make soup go further,
add wine, cream or stock. This will enhance the taste as well.

You can disguise gravy made from instant granules
by stirring in one main flavour; for example, some apple juice for pork or a tin of chopped tomatoes for lamb.

Has a vegetarian turned up without warning?

Don't fret. Take a tin of baked beans, stir in some wine and pour the mixture over a selection of your vegetables. Bake it in the oven for 20 minutes while you recover from the shock with a glass of wine. Result – one tasty vegetable bake and a happy guest.

If an extra guest turns up,

most things can be stretched into casseroles. Salmon steaks can be flaked and covered with a sauce; meat and vegetables can be put into a stewing dish.

If you're tight for oven space

all meats can be half cooked one day before and then finished off when needed.

Rice is one of the most common culinary disasters.

Make yours well in advance if you're having a dinner party. Then, before it's quite done, turn off the heat. Leave the lid on and it will retain its heat whilst also losing some of its stodginess.

Presentation is everything.

Some fresh herbs sprinkled onto the top of the most ordinary looking dish will turn it into something special.

Tie your tools down!

When you throw a party, tie the bottle opener and cork screw onto a long length of string attached to something immovable. They have a habit of disappearing just when you need them.

Why risk your own glasses?

All drinks retailers now provide free glass hire when you buy your booze from them.

Remember the 'designated drivers'
and non-drinkers. Always have enough soft drinks. Try mixing fruit juice with mineral water rather than just having lots of fizzy drinks. If you have the time, some pretty non-alcoholic cocktails will make the abstemious feel their drink is still special.

Make drinks fun
by adding food colouring.

It's difficult to judge how much people will drink,
so for a big event buy your drink on a use or return basis. Be on the safe side and order more than you think you'll need.

To avoid wax on your tablecloths,
put a beer mat under the candles.

Always set your dining room table with candles.
Apart from looking pretty, they disperse strong smells.

To make candles burn brightly,
soak the wicks in vinegar.

If you get candle wax on your tablecloth,
heat a spoon over the candle. Then place a piece of wet newspaper over the wax and rub the hot spoon over the newspaper to melt the wax which will then come off the tablecloth and stick to the paper.

To make your candles burn for longer,
freeze them first.

To transform instant coffee into a more sophisticated offering,
add a few cardamom seeds. Serve the coffee black... and remember to remove the seeds before serving!

To bring out the taste of fresh coffee,
>add a pinch of dried mustard powder to the percolator.

Inexpensive firelighters
>can be created from the stubs of burnt-down candles, orange peel or matchboxes filled with used matches and a bit of candle wax. Waxed milk cartons are excellent for bigger blazes.

Once your fire is going,
>a few digestive biscuits thrown in make it burn like fury.

For a pretty Christmas napkin ring,
>dry a slice of orange with the middle cut out.

Keep your mineral water fizzy;
>give the plastic bottle a good squeeze before screwing the top back on.

Always store cooked foods above uncooked food
> in a fridge to avoid raw juices dripping onto cooked food... that's the quickest way to dangerous food contamination.

When freezing big bags of ice,
> sprinkle the cubes with some soda water to stop them all sticking together in clumps.

You can bring water to the boil
> much more quickly if you place the lid on the pan and then put a large scoop of salt on top of the lid.

To cook rice, soak in cold water for an hour or two first.
> This saves you time and fuel in the long run.

Remember,
> the best chefs always use the freshest ingredients.

To reduce the need for artificial lights,
make sure you clean the windows
thoroughly – dirty windows can reduce
the natural light by around 20 per cent.

Brazil nuts are easier to crack
when frozen in the freezer.

Make consommé look more appetizing
– drop a lump of sugar into the soup
before serving.

Keep flowers fresh for longer
– add a splash of lemonade to the vase.

It really is simple to impress your guests
with hot cleansing towels after a dinner
party. Just wet some clean flannels with
water and a splash of eau-de-Cologne,
loosely wrap in cling film and heat
in the microwave for about a minute.
Throw them all into a pretty basket
and pass around your friends.

For a quick party dip,
> beat milk and onion powder into Philadelphia cheese until you have your required consistency.

To make a tasty dip
> for guests, mix half a packet of mushroom or onion soup with a small carton of cream and chill for a few hours.

Scoop out green or red peppers
> to make containers for mayonnaise, salad dressings, sauces and dips.

For a special custard for adults,
> pour in a small glassful of apricot or cherry brandy just before serving.

Add a touch of luxury to coffee
> with a teaspoon of vanilla ice-cream instead of milk.

Surprise guests?
No desserts? Take two ginger biscuits and sandwich them together with some gently whipped cream. Serve with coffee.

To chill beer, wine or champagne quickly,
add about five tablespoons of salt to the ice and water in the ice bucket. The bottles should chill in about 20 minutes.

To stop last-minute panics
at dinner parties – boil your vegetables in advance, then run them under the cold-water tap. Just before serving, boil the kettle and pour the boiling water over the vegetables. Leave for thirty seconds and serve.

Before serving cheese at a dinner party,
warm the cheese knife in the oven. This makes it easier for the knife to cut through the cheese and it spares your guests the embarrassment of struggling to cut the cheese.

Keep picnic food cool on a hot day.
Put the food in a bowl. Take a larger bowl and put ice in the bottom. Then put the smaller bowl inside the larger one – a portable refrigerator!

Add a measure of Baileys Irish Cream
to custard for a really special flavour.

Experimenting with new ingredients?
To test ingredients before adding them to the mix, take a spoonful of the dish and add a drop of the ingredient to be added for tasting rather than risking spoiling the whole.

To keep bread rolls warm,
line a bread basket with foil and then cover the rolls with a napkin.

You'll find party sandwiches stay fresh
if you place paper napkins over them and sprinkle with cold water regularly.

You can't beat serving refreshing iced tea
>or coffee to guests when it's hot. Why not freeze any left-overs from your usual brew in ice-cube trays. You'll have plenty of ice to chill your drinks without diluting them.

When serving something cold like paté
>or ice-cream or a cold soup, always add lots of flavourings as the cold will numb the palette.

Use music to change the mood when entertaining.
>Something pacy will get you moving in the kitchen then slow things down with something relaxing so you can enjoy your meal with everyone else.

For comfortable guests,
>remember to set your heating thermostat a few degrees lower than usual. All those bodies will create their own heat.

If you're having a party,
set up drinks in a different corner to the food so that people aren't climbing on top of each other – it will also encourage guests to 'circulate'.

Don't feel you have to do all the cooking for a dinner party.
If your guests ask if they can bring anything, suggest they bring a pudding – some lovely fresh cream cakes, Danish pastries or pâtisserie will go down a treat!

For a sweet treat at a barbecue
bring out a couple of bags of marshmallows for toasting on the hot coals.

Warm plates for a dinner party
in the drying cycle of your dishwasher.

Caviare must be served on cold toast
– hot toast will make the eggs separate.

FEEDING CHILDREN

*'A child should always say what's true
and speak when he is spoken to
And behave mannerly at table
At least as far as he is able.'*
Robert Louis Stevenson

Savoury

Every one to his taste.
Proverb

When babies are first weaned onto solids,
they only want a tiny bit each time. Avoid waste and make life more convenient by making up large batches of fresh vegetables or fruit then purée them into ice-cube trays to use as needed.

Be patient!
Start off with one or two teaspoons of food a day. Don't make a big issue of it or you could end up with a fussy eater. If your baby isn't interested, go back to milk for a day or so and then try again.

Take one step at a time
and introduce new foods one by one. That way, you can detect if your child is allergic to anything specific.

Save time and cook for the whole family in one go.

You don't need to cook twice; just cook the 'grown-up' food without seasoning, put a little to one side and purée it. Then season your own food the way you like it.

When your children want to start feeding themselves,

dress them in a painting overall rather than a normal feeding bib – it will cover much more of their clothes and is waterproof so it will save on laundry too. Believe me, the mess can be quite outrageous!

Faddy eaters

may be encouraged to eat if you make meal-times fun. Arrange food to create patterns and shapes or to spell out their name.

Try arranging finger foods

in the different compartments of an ice-cube tray – children love 'little things'.

When serving soup to children,
stir an ice cube into their portions to cool it down quickly.

A fun way to encourage children to eat
their dinner is to give them chop-sticks instead of knives and forks. (Not for the faint hearted or anyone with a new carpet.)

Get the kids cooking
but don't give them sharp kitchen implements. They can use plastic knives and forks instead.

To make cooking fun for kids,
let them press all the buttons (on the blender, oven etc.) while you do the boring stuff of removing all the hot food.

For a healthy and tasty pizza
with a difference, spread some marmite onto a pizza base before adding favourite toppings.

To create fun-shaped sandwiches
for children use metal pastry cutters.

Children thrive on routine in their daily activities.
Try to serve meals at the same time each day.

Eating is a new experience for small children.
Don't be surprised if at first a child is cautious and curious, plays with food, is reluctant to try new foods and rebels when forced to eat. Try to be patient, relax and maintain a sense of humour – even if they appear to be eating nothing, you'll be surprised how much actually goes in during a day.

Snacks are not always bad for children.
Nutritious snack foods can help children to obtain required nutrients. Since children have smaller stomachs than adults, they are natural grazers – so serving three small meals with a nourishing snack in between each meal may be more appropriate than serving three large meals.

But – frequent snacking
> may contribute to tooth decay.
> Clean children's teeth each day and
> check with a dentist about the need
> for fluoride.

Children often want to eat one certain food at every opportunity.
> This is called a food jag and typically
> occurs among toddlers. As long as the
> preferred food is nutritious and the jag
> does not last long, there is nothing to
> worry about. If you go along with it, the
> child will probably get bored of the food
> soon enough.

Children's appetites
> may suddenly decrease around the age
> of two due to a decrease in their growth
> rate. As growth slows down, energy
> requirements are also reduced. So
> don't worry if a previously hungry
> hippo turns into a nibbling mouse!

Don't face children with huge helpings

– they'll eat much better if confronted with an obviously manageable portion and, if they then eat a second helping, they'll feel a real sense of achievement!

Slice frankfurters

into four strips lengthwise and then cut into small pieces which can't block the windpipe and cause the child to choke.

Cook meat at a low temperature

(300–325 °F/150–160 °C/Gas Mark 2–3) to keep it tender and juicy. We all remember chewing on a mouthful of meat which just wouldn't go away!

When children are first learning to feed themselves,

cut meat into small julienne strips that can be picked up and eaten by hand. Older children who are using tableware still need to have their meat cut into bite-size pieces with the fat and gristle trimmed to prevent choking.

Children usually enjoy brightly coloured

fruits and vegetables.

Children like their vegetables crunchy,

not soft. Vegetables steamed in a small amount of water, microwaved or stir-fried are not only crisp, but retain most of their colour, flavour and nutrients far better than boiled ones.

Many strong vegetables

such as cabbage, turnip, cauliflower, spinach, broccoli and asparagus are very acceptable to children when served with grated cheese or a cheese sauce.

Avoid giving raw carrots
and whole peas, corn and grapes to children under four years old to prevent choking. Cook and mash carrots, corn and peas, and cut grapes into quarters.

Many older children
enjoy raw vegetables served with their own individual bowl of dip.

When shopping with children,
encourage them to help select fruits and vegetables, especially ones they have never tried before.

Taste food
before adding butter, margarine, dressing, jellies and jams. Since children follow the example of adults, limit your own use of fats and sugars, and use only moderate amounts of these foods in meal preparation.

Seat children at a table
for meals and snacks, and discourage them from eating while walking or standing.

Cover the floor
directly under a child's seat with paper, vinyl or plastic.

Purchase a spoon or fork
with a short, straight, broad, solid handle; the spoon should have a wide mouth and the fork should have blunt prongs. Children will begin to feed themselves with a spoon and will learn to use a fork later.

Place food at the level of a child's stomach,
where it is less tiring for a child to reach.

Children playing with food
should be allowed to leave the table rather than disturb others. This usually indicates that a child has had enough to eat. Don't encourage children to clean their plates when they're no longer hungry. This may lead to overeating or the development of an aversion to food.

Sometimes children behave better
and enjoy meal-time more when they sit down to a meal with the family at a nicely set table. Allowing older children to have candles makes a meal into a special occasion, and little ones can help to blow them out when everyone's eaten well.

Encourage children to try at least one bite of a new food.
If after one bite children reject it, reintroduce the food later.

Allow children to eat at their friends' homes.
>These visits offer an excellent opportunity for them to try new foods. Try incorporating these new foods into the meals you prepare.

Start nutrition education early
>by explaining the function of nutrients found in common foods (e.g. milk makes bones and teeth strong).

Meal preparation should not be a burden.
>Salads, raw vegetables, fruits and ready-to-serve meats, fish and cheese are nutritious and easy to prepare.

Breakfasts don't have to be traditional.
>Any nutritious combination of foods from all food groups is recommended. Incorporate left-overs when preparing breakfast.

Encourage children to participate in quiet activities before a meal-time.
>It's difficult to get an excited child to settle down to eat.

Feed children before guests arrive.

Children require a lot of attention at meal-time and it may be impossible to give it to them while entertaining guests.

Children's blood-sugar levels often run low quite quickly.

If your toddlers suddenly seem irritable for no apparent reason, try giving them a little bit of fruit or cheese.

Boring bites can be transformed into magical meals

with a few drops of food colouring and a little imagination. Mashed potato can become green grass or blue sea, pasta can be colourful snakes, and rice can be any colour of the rainbow. Even the humble egg boiled in its shell can become jewel red or sunshine yellow. Choose your child's favourite colour and they'll soon start eating up.

Whenever they eat, children should be sitting upright,
not lying down or running around. Always supervise at snack and mealtimes, because a child who is choking cannot make noise to attract your attention. Coughing, on the other hand, is a sign that the child is removing the obstacle naturally. Before intervening, give the child the chance to cough out the food.

The grinding action of a child's teeth is not very effective
until at least four years of age. Because of this, foods that are hard or tough to chew, small and round or sticky are more likely to cause choking. These foods include: frankfurters, raw apples, candy, raw carrots, nuts, corn, grapes, peas, popcorn, chunks of meat, raisins, and all types of peanut butter spread too thickly.

When travelling by car,
bus or train with young children, consider their special needs. Always pack snacks when taking a trip that will last longer than one hour.

Be sure to keep hot foods hot
and cold foods cold. A cooler, which can be stored in a car or below the seat of a bus or train, will allow you to pack a variety of foods.

Pack tableware,
napkins, moist towelettes or a washcloth that has been moistened and stored in a plastic bag.

Raw vegetables,
fruits, cheese, crackers and tubes of yoghurt are easily eaten in a car, and store well. Pack cheese, cold cuts, peanut butter, jelly and a loaf of bread to make sandwiches on an extra long trip.

When travelling by plane,
don't expect the airlines to cater for the needs of children, although they sometimes do. Today, many airlines are limiting their meal service in order to reduce air fares. It's usually a good idea to bring along sandwiches, fruit, cheese, crackers and raw vegetables, which can be kept for a short period of time without refrigeration. Even though airlines usually provide beverages during a flight, you may want to bring a thermos of milk or cans of juice to prevent children from getting fussy. There will be so much new going on around them, at least the food and drink can be familiar.

Pay attention to the special needs of children
when dining with them at restaurants. If you must wait before being seated, take children for a walk outside the restaurant to prevent them from becoming impatient.

Some children expect to eat as soon as they sit

at a dinner table and will fill up on appetizers and bread, leaving no room for their main meal. Try to prevent this by asking the waiter or waitress not to put out the bread in advance of the meal. When you order, inquire about children's size portions.

Young children will feel more at home in a restaurant

if you bring along their cups and tableware.

Children involved in meal preparation

develop a more active interest in food. They can accomplish many different tasks when working one-on-one with an adult in the kitchen. Having patience and time to spend with children when involving them in meal preparation is the key to success.

Two and three year olds
>need to learn about personal hygiene – encourage them to wash their hands before handling any food or eating.

But they love having 'jobs' to do.
>Try asking them to wash vegetables, wipe the table, tear lettuce, help to shape burgers and meatballs, peel bananas (if the top has been started) and clear their own place setting.

Three and four year olds
>like to feel challenged. Let them break eggs into a bowl, measure and mix ingredients, knead and shape dough, pour their own cereal out and toss salads.

Five year olds
>can make cakes and cookies using baking mixes, help make pancakes, French toast, scrambled eggs, hot cereal and rice (with close supervision), set and clear the table and load the dishwasher.

Encourage the teenagers
>to help out in the kitchen. Put up a notice each day saying what's for dinner. If they get home before you they will know which vegetables to start chopping or to preheat the oven. You may even find dinner waiting for you. (But don't bank on it...!)

Sweet

'Food Glorious Food!'
Charles Dickens

For healthy ice-lollies
>that will still please little ones, top and tail a pineapple and cut downwards into about six chunky wedges, then freeze.

Give the kids a treat
>with home-made, creamy, banana ice-lollies. Blend a banana with some milk, then pour into moulds, add a stick and freeze.

When making your own ice-lollies,
> put any piece of real fruit in to pep up the taste and make them healthy.

To remove home-made ice-lollies
> from their mould, place the mould under running warm water.

Keep insects out of children's drinks
> when having a picnic. Cover the tops of beakers with cling film and push a straw through.

Children will love bananas
> if you coat them in melted chocolate and roll them in coconut.

Dilute pure fruit juice
> with sparkling mineral water when serving to children.

Give kids small cups to drink from
> – they're easier to carry and therefore less likely to be dropped. If they do get dropped, there's less to clean up.

Do your kids' hands get messy

when eating ice-lollies? Just take a disc of card, put the stick of the lolly through the card and, as the lolly melts, the juices will drip on to the card and not on to the children's hands.

For fun cup cakes,

top with a marshmallow a couple of minutes before removing from the oven.

Children don't usually like ice-cold milk.

Try pouring it a short time before serving to take off the chill.

Serve milk in plastic cups

with covers that fit or unbreakable cups with weighted bottoms. Fill cups half-way to make milk more difficult to spill; this will also make the task of drinking milk seem less awesome.

Only offer flavoured milk on special occasions.
> Children should develop a taste for plain milk, which has fewer calories than flavoured.

If children refuse to drink milk,
> try to include milk-based soups, cottage cheese, yoghurt, cheese, custard or cereal with milk in their diets.

If a child is over age two,
> serve low-fat milk rather than whole-fat milk.

Young children
> often prefer the taste of bland sweet fruits to tart fruits. Serve tart fruits from time to time to develop a child's taste for all fruit.

Peel, core and seed fruit
> for very young children. Fresh, dried, canned and frozen fruits and juices make nutritious snacks and desserts.

To reduce the chance of cavities,
> clean children's teeth with a moistened washcloth or gauze, especially after they have eaten dried fruits.

Do not offer sweets as a bribe
> or withhold them as punishment.

Since children know that sweets do exist,
> serving sweets on special occasions may be a more sensible approach than excluding them completely. By sometimes including them in your child's diet, you avoid making them into a big deal.

While you should avoid
> feeding gumdrops, jelly beans, hard candy, nuts and popcorn to very young children, many other childhood favourites can still be enjoyed.

Milk and fruit juices

are more nutritious than soft drinks and can be stored in a cooler or thermos. Juice will remain cold if you slightly freeze individual cans before packing.

Put the sweets in the freezer

for a couple of hours. The paper should peel off easily and the sweets won't be too sticky for little fingers.

TOOLS OF
THE TRADE

'They say everything in the world is good for something.'
The Spanish Friar, **Dryden**

For a great rolling pin,
>fill a claret bottle with warm water and replace the cork.

If you haven't got a pastry cutter,
>use the cleaned lid of an aerosol can instead.

It's easier to cut pizza
>with scissors than a knife.

If you don't have a cake tin with a removable base,
>don't worry. Grease your tin as normal. Cut a long strip of kitchen foil and put it into the bottom of the tin so that each end of the foil strip goes up the side and hangs over the edge. Put a circle of greaseproof paper in the bottom and fill with the cake mixture. When you need to get the cake out, gently lift it using the foil tabs.

If you don't have a turntable for decorating a cake,

don't worry. Take two plates, sandwich them together back to back with a little cooking oil and place on a damp tea towel to stop the bottom plate slipping. Placed on top, your cake will turn round beautifully.

Before using a new baking tin,

line it with some grease and bake it in a very hot oven for at least ten minutes. Wash as normal in soapy water and you'll find your tin stays as good as new for ages.

Royal icing

is notoriously difficult to beat with a food mixer. Try fixing the whisk attachment to a variable-speed drill instead.

No piping bag?

Just twist some foil into a cone and snip off the bottom.

Keep your wooden chopping block clean.
Just wash it down when you've finished butchering and then cover with sawdust. This soaks up the damp and the resin in the block kills off any bacteria.

To sharpen a knife with a serrated edge,
just sharpen with a steel on the serrated side (not both sides).

Keep a carbon-steel knife clean
by dipping a cork in scouring powder and running it along the side of the blade. Rinse the knife, dry it and wipe it down with vegetable oil.

To clean up any spills in the oven,
sprinkle some salt and cinnamon over the mess. This stops the house from filling with that acrid smoky smell and the spill will be easy to lift off with a spatula.

To clean an aluminum pan,
boil the peel of an apple in some water. This will make it much easier to clean the pan afterwards.

To clean a grater,
>rub a hard crust of bread over it.

Keep your knives nice and rust-free
>– plunge them into an onion and leave there for half an hour. Wash and then polish lightly with some vegetable oil.

If you need both hands free to pour and press when sieving,
>remove the top and bottom of a large tin with a can opener and place over a bowl as a rest for the sieve.

To loosen a tight jar lid,
>wind an elastic band around it to form a great grip.

To remove air from freezer bags,
>use a bicycle pump.

There's nothing worse than a really stale smelling fridge.
>Put a few charcoal bricks at the back to keep it smelling fresh and clean.

Alternatively,
> take an orange and stick some cloves in it. Placed in your fridge, it will keep it sweet for weeks.

Also,
> to make your fridge smell clean and fresh, squeeze lemon juice on to cotton wool balls, place them in a perforated freezer bag and pop inside the door of the fridge.

Before boiling milk,
> dampen the bottom of the pan with water. When the milk boils, it won't burn the bottom.

To clean a really rusty knife,
> cut a potato in half and dip it in bicarbonate of soda. Rub the potato hard on both sides of the blade for a gleaming finish.

When chopping,
> put a damp tea towel under your chopping board to give it a firm grip on the table.

When cooking in a microwave,
>paper coffee filters make excellent lids for bowls and dishes.

To cut the perfect slice of paté or gateaux,
>first run the knife blade under very hot water.

To prevent your wok from going rusty,
>dry it thoroughly every time you use it. Rub it with oil and salt and always store it in a dry place away from water, steam and condensation.

Save time and energy
>by placing a large dish at the bottom of your oven. It will catch any spills and will wash up easily, leaving you with a lovely clean oven.

To help your fridge last that bit longer
>don't open and close it unnecessarily. Otherwise, you will make the fridge motor work twice as hard and wear out twice as fast.

To stop your bins from smelling unpleasant,
   throw a few fresh herbs in each time you throw something away.

Or,
   try keeping half a lemon on the bottom of the bin.

Keep teapots smelling fresh
   – put a sugar lump or dry tea bag inside it until you want to use it.

A few grains of rice in the salt cellar
   will ensure it stays dry and fresh.

To keep brown sugar really fresh,
   put a small piece of brown bread in with the sugar.

Dirty ashtrays look so ugly.
   Keep them clean with an old shaving brush.

To make your plates gleam like new,
   rinse them in a weak solution of water and vinegar.

Good quality china
> will really sparkle if soaked in water with denture-cleaning tablets.

Kill off dangerous germs lingering on kitchen cloths
> – heat damp cloths for several minutes in a microwave.

Don't despair if you burn a pan
> boil up some sliced onions and water, and leave for several hours.

Alternatively,
> you could boil up some water and vinegar in a burnt pan and leave it overnight. It will be easier to clean in the morning.

If you have a discoloured aluminum pan,
> boil up a weak solution of rhubarb or tomatoes in it. The food acids lift the stain.

To clean hard baked-on food from a cooking pan,
put a sheet of fabric conditioner in the pan and fill with water. Leave overnight and the next day the food will just lift off with a sponge.

Polish up cutlery using a cork
soaked in water and scouring powder. Rinse and buff with a soft cloth.

Clean a grotty roasting tin
(not aluminum or non-stick) with a solution of washing soda and water boiled up in the tin. Rinse and then dry in a cool oven.

To stop dishes like lasagne
and cottage pie sticking to the baking tin, grease with butter and line with breadcrumbs.

If you always get in a mess with cling film,
try storing it in the fridge. It's easier to use when cold.

To prevent scrambled eggs sticking
> to the pan add two tablespoons of cold water per half dozen eggs.

To stop honey or syrup sticking to your spoon,
> grease it first with a little oil.

Also,
> try dipping the spoon in boiling water before you dip it in the honey.

Clean old Pringles boxes and use them to store biscuits.
> The smaller boxes are ideal for children's school snacks.

Some foods like bacon and rhubarb can be difficult to chop
> – try using scissors instead of a knife.

If you need to cover a saucepan
> or wok use kitchen foil as a lid. It can be used several times.

The waxed bags inside cereal boxes
> make excellent linings for your cake tins.

Line kitchen scales with cling film
before weighing out ingredients, so you don't need to wash them afterwards. When weighing sticky butter, this means the correct amount makes it into the mixture rather than staying in the scales!

Don't throw away foil trays from take-aways
– wash them and keep them to use as mini baking trays.

To get rid of the starch
that rises to the top of the pan when cooking rice, hold a cold serving spoon so that it rests on the surface of the water and most of the starch will stick to the bottom of the spoon.

Barbecue charcoal
is ready for cooking on when 80 per cent is covered with grey ash.

Keep a scrapbook of recipes cut out of magazines,
papers and from packets.

To restore the white to a plastic chopping board,
>rub with half a lemon and wash in warm water.

To clean coffee pots,
>put in some ice cubes and some salt and swirl round.

To shine the bottom of copper pans,
>rub with half a lemon and some salt.

To remove burnt food
>from the bottom of casserole dishes, cover the mess with baking powder and fill with warm water. Leave to stand for ten minutes and the food will come off without any hassle.

When making pizzas or bread at home,
>create an brick oven-baked flavour. Buy some terracotta tiles from a DIY store. Place a layer of the tiles on an oven shelf. Preheat the oven and place the pizza or bread directly on to the tiles to cook.

To keep a mixing bowl in place
> without having to hold it, take a wet kitchen towel and twist it into a ring-shape. Wrap the towel around the bottom of the bowl.

If your pan looks like it's about to boil over,
> put a whisk in and beat quickly. The bubbles will go down like magic.

When a recipe calls for a coating of oil,
> it's really hard to make that coating even. So, try pouring some oil into a spray bottle. Hold it about a foot from the food and spray.

To remove burnt food from the bottom of pans,
> wet a cloth in boiling water and then leave it stretched over the top of the pan for half an hour. Then clean the pan thoroughly.

To save energy,
> use the smallest pans you can – less metal, less energy needed to heat it up. (And less time to wash up afterwards!)

Copper-bottomed pans
heat more quickly than other types of pans.

To save pennies in the kitchen...
if you have electric rings on your cooker, turn them off a minute or so before cooking is complete. The rings will stay hot enough to continue to cook the food.

Microwaves
cook more efficiently if the inside is clean.

To prevent wooden kebab skewers charring in the oven,
soak them in water for 20 minutes before cooking.

To check whether the fat
in your deep-fat fryer is hot enough to start cooking, drop a popcorn kernel into the fat. When the kernel pops, the fat is hot enough to start cooking in.

Tomato ketchup has a clever second use

– to clean the base of copper-bottomed pans. Pour some over the bottom of the pan and leave for a few minutes. Then rub the ketchup in and wash it off.

To stop the bottom of a pan scratching

the inside of the one it is stacked on top of, put the lid of a margarine tub inside the larger pan as a 'cushion'.

To avoid cutting the ends of your fingers

when grating cheese, wear thimbles.

To make a more imaginative basting brush,

take sprigs of fresh herbs and bind them together to make a brush. When you use it to baste, the taste of the herbs will transfer to the meat.

To make filling up piping bags easier,

stand the bag in a tall glass. Fold the edges of the bag over the top of the glass and fill. Easy!

To make cleaning a cheese grater easier,
after grating the cheese, grate a raw potato. The potato will clear the cheesy gunk from the holes.

Use different sides of the chopping boards
for different things – one for things with strong odours and one for things that you don't want to be affected by strong odours. Write on the board (with an indelible felt-tip pen) what each side is for.

Slicing kiwis is easy
– just use an egg-slicer. Remove the skin from the slice of kiwi by edging a teaspoon around between the flesh and the skin.

Never store vinegar in a metal container.
The acidity will affect the metal.

Never cover an entire oven rack in foil.
It stops the air circulating so your food will take longer to cook.

Different types of baking dish produce different results.

Dark, dull pans produce crispy crusts (so suitable for pies); shinier ones give more delicate results (so good for cakes).

To make cutting raisins

and other sticky things easier, coat the blade of your knife with vegetable oil.

To keep fruit and veg in your fridge nice and fresh,

place a dry sponge at the bottom of the salad drawer – it will absorb excess moisture and stop food going rotten.

Store kitchen bits and bobs

like piping bag ends in empty film canisters to avoid losing them.

Re-use good quality storage bags

– just wash thoroughly and dry.

Plastic containers

from your supermarket are great for storing herbs and left-overs, or for freezing stock.

A simple way to remove a frozen dessert

or jelly from a mould is to loosen the edges with the point of a knife and give the mould a blast with a hair-dryer for a few seconds.

If you keep salt for seasoning

in a small bowl instead of a shaker or grinder you'll be less likely to over salt a dish as you'll have total control over the amount you use.

When tasting food during preparation,

fill your tasting spoon from your stirring spoon – to avoid your germs being transferred back into the food.

If you've got no time for sifting,

put all your dry ingredients in a bowl and stir briskly with a whisk.

An egg-slicer
   is perfect for slicing mushrooms.

Keep a spray bottle
   filled with water handy when grilling, to douse any flare ups.

Filter coffee
   left-overs are excellent for removing grease from stainless steel.

If you want beautiful smooth icing
   on a cake try using an artist's paint scraper.

For uniform hamburgers,
   meatballs etc. use an ice-cream scoop.

As a rule, sharp knives are safer
   than blunt ones.

If you want perfect cheese curls
   try using a potato peeler.

To make neat butter curls,
> freeze the butter for a few minutes first.

If your bread wrapper has melted on to a hot toaster
> don't worry, rub the mark with nail-polish remover for spotless results.

Wipe bicarbonate of soda on the inside of the oven
> and the oven will be less likely to get dirty.

To avoid frozen foods
> that you buy from a supermarket thawing out before you get them home, pick them up last so you don't carry them around the supermarket while you get your other shopping.

Try to draw up your shopping list
> in the order that you reach the appropriate aisles in the supermarket. That way, you're less likely to waste time criss-crossing the supermarket.

To remember which cans of food
you need to replace when you go shopping, put labels on the wall of your shelves to indicate where particular cans are stored ('canned tomatoes', 'baked beans', etc.). When you use the last can, it will reveal the label and tell you that you need to get another one.

To avoid forgetting regular items
when you go shopping, type a list on to a computer and save. Then, each week, add one-off items and re-print.

When you're cooking from a recipe book,
cover the open page with some cling film to stop it getting marked.

Laying the table for a special occasion?
Add some perfume to the candles for an aromatic delight.

You don't need expensive silver napkin rings. Try tying the napkins with some pretty ribbons. You can be even more imaginative – for a summer barbecue try tying some garden twine around paper towels with a bay leaf or lavender stem tucked inside each.

BAKING AND SWEETS

The way to a man's heart is through his stomach.
Proverb

Bread

Bread is the staff of Life.
Proverb

Have a couple of small freezer bags ready
> when baking so you can pop them over your floury hands if the 'phone rings to stop the flour messing up the receiver!

The secret of fantastic bread
> is to always keep a little bit of dough back from the previous day's batch and add it to the new mixture.

If you can't remember whether you've added yeast to your dough,
> here's a simple test. Take out a small piece of the dough – about gobstopper size – and put it in a cup of hot water. If you didn't put in any yeast, it will immediately sink to the bottom. Dough with yeast in it will rise to the top.

To make authentic-tasting naan
or pitta bread, gently warm the flour in a microwave first.

The longer you knead dough,
the longer you should leave it to develop.

To prevent bread from drying out when baking,
cover it with a cake tin in the oven.

Stop gaping air pockets developing during baking
– soak some breadcrumbs in water and sprinkle them into your meat pies.

Dried out, stale bread
can be revived if you wrap it in kitchen foil and leave it on a low heat in the oven for about ten minutes.

To keep bread moist
while baking, add a little honey to the dough.

To keep home-baked bread fresh for longer,
add a couple of teaspoons of vegetable oil to the dough.

Stop mice or mites getting to your flour
– put a bay leaf in the packet.

Store flour in the freezer
to make it last for longer.

To stop garlic bread going soggy
during cooking, wrap it in tin foil.

When kneading dough,
stop every two or three minutes to let the dough 'rest'. After resting for a couple of minutes, the dough will be easier to knead.

Flour compacts during storage.
Fluff it up before measuring out an amount for a recipe or you'll get too much flour.

If, when heating or baking bread at home,
the bread starts to burn, cut off the burnt spots and brush them with beaten egg. Then keep heating the bread.

To revitalize stale bread,
plunge the loaf or rolls into cold water for a moment and then bake on a low heat for ten minutes.

To remove crusts from bread,
try using a pizza cutter, it will give you a nice neat edge and waste less.

To test whether a loaf of home-made bread
is baked properly, tap it on top. A hollow sound means that it is baked.

Place a wet towel over your dough
when making bread, to make it rise more quickly.

Pies, Flans and Pizzas

'Tis an ill cook that cannot lick his own fingers.'
Romeo and Juliet, William Shakespeare

When rolling pastry,
put it between two sheets of cling film. You won't need to use extra flour to stop it sticking to the surfaces and it is easier to turn around.

Also,
don't turn your body at an angle when rolling out pastry. Turn the pastry round so that you don't hurt your back.

You can roll pastry of a uniform thickness
by using two bits of wood either side of the pastry and running the rolling pin across the top of the wood.

Always let pie pastry dry
> thoroughly before adding the pie filling. This way a skin forms so the mixture doesn't seep in during cooking.

Put sugar in a pie,
> not on it, for a much more even flavour. Anyway, sugar on a pie often burns.

When trimming pie edges,
> cut the pastry outwards on the dish, not inwards, to make the pastry grip the edge of the dish.

When slicing apples
> for pies, place them in some salted water to stop them discolouring until you're ready to use them.

For better-tasting apple pies,
> add cloves to the pastry not the filling. When the pie is baked, it is much easier to find and remove cloves from the pastry than from the filling.

For savoury pies,
> add a little pesto to flavour the pastry – delicious!

Before putting puff pastry on a baking tray,
> run the tray under ice-cold water. When the tray is in the oven, the steam rising from it will help the pastry to puff!

When cooking vol-au-vents,
> don't put them in really straight lines on your baking tray. Instead, place them randomly but close together and they will lift each other up while cooking.

To store vol-au-vents,
> sprinkle a thin layer of salt on the bottom of a cake tin, cover with a tea towel and place your vol-au-vents on the cloth. They will stay fresh for ages.

Make a quiche without the hassle or calories of pastry
> – simply bake the mixture in a lightly oiled, shallow casserole dish.

To prevent soggy quiche bases,
> brush the pastry with lemon juice and bake for three minutes before putting the filling in and cooking fully.

To stop the base and crust of fruit pies
> going soggy during cooking, sprinkle the pastry with flour before putting in the filling.

To stop pastry sticking to your rolling pin,
> put the pin in the freezer or fridge until it's cold and then start rolling.

When you've cooked berries for pie fillings,
> save any left-over juice for topping pancakes and ice-cream.

To avoid soggy pie crusts,
> sprinkle a layer of breadcrumbs over them before cooking.

If, midway through cooking a fruit pie,
> you notice that the fruit is seeping out, sprinkle salt over the leaking fruit. The fruit will become crisp and can easily be removed.

To refresh dried-out mincemeat
> (for mince pies), add brandy or sherry.

To warm bowls that can't go in the oven,
> fill them with boiling water and leave to stand for five minutes. Then pour away the water, dry the bowl and serve...

Left-over mashed potato
> is wonderful in pastry dishes, adding a lovely flavour and texture.

To stop frozen pizzas sticking
> to the tray or foil during cooking and to make them taste nicer, brush the base with olive oil.

Some pizza take-aways
sell off uncollected orders for a reduced price.

Make sweet pizzas
– use fruit as a topping and even jam instead of tomato paste.

Never run out of breadcrumbs for stuffings and toppings
– keep all your bread ends, pop them into a food processor to make crumbs and then freeze them in bags.

Try using a packet of stuffing
instead of breadcrumbs on scotch eggs for a tasty change.

Biscuits and Cakes

'Pat a cake, Pat a cake...'
Traditional Nursery Rhyme

If you're baking shortbread cookies,
try substituting half of your plain flour with corn-flour for a really rich taste and extra crispy cookies.

To stop cake mix sticking
to your spoon when you're transferring it to a tin, try dipping the spoon in milk beforehand.

Save time when making biscuits
– instead of cutting lots of individual round shapes, just roll the dough into a sausage shape and cut slices off it.

Don't rush to get your scones in the oven.
Resting them allows the baking powder to become active.

To make shortbread
with that delicious luxury taste, add a tablespoon of custard powder to the raw mix per batch of 24.

Also, custard powder
added to a basic sponge mixture will give the cake a wonderful golden glow.

When making cakes,
leave the eggs and fat out overnight before so that they all reach the same temperature.

Make sure any essence
you use adds flavour to the whole cake – mix it in one of the eggs before adding to the mixture.

Your cakes will never stick
if you use olive oil to grease the tins.

To cut a sponge cake horizontally,
take two pieces of wood of equal thickness and of half the depth of the cake, and lie them either side of the cake. Slide the knife in a sawing action across the top of the wood and through the cake.

Do your cakes always sink?
It's not necessarily the opening of the oven door that does it but the closing. If you don't do it very gently, the sudden movement can cause the cake to sink.

To stop the fruit in cakes from sinking,
first wash it then coat in glycerine.

To stop glacé cherries from sinking,
coat them lightly in flour before using.

For a really moist fruit cake,
use marmalade instead of candied peel.

Always soak dried fruit overnight
– for extra flavour, soak the fruit in apple or orange juice.

For a special occasion cake,
>   marinate the fruit in your favourite liqueur the week before.

If your cakes always come out cracked,
>   put a dish of cold water in the bottom of the oven before baking.

Before sandwiching your cake
>   together with jam, spread a little butter on each sponge surface. This will prevent the cake absorbing all the jam.

Use muslin instead of a sieve
>   to dust over a doily with icing sugar. It is much finer and the effect is so much prettier.

If you want your cake to have a flat top
>   for decorating, spoon out a bit of the mixture from the middle of the tin before baking.

To dry a cake out,
>   put it under an angle-poise desk lamp.

Before icing a cake,
sprinkle the top with some flour; this will stop the icing running down over the edges.

For a deceptively clever effect,
put two colours of icing in a bag and then pipe out. The two-tone result is stunning.

Glacé icings can be horribly sweet.
Substituting the water with milk will give a lovely creamy texture and reduce the sweetness.

To keep cakes fresh in the tin,
throw in half an apple.

To spot whether an egg is absolutely fresh,
put it in a bowl of water. If it is really fresh, it will sink to the bottom. Older eggs float to the top.

To de-stone cherries,
use a hair grip stuck into a cork.

To prevent jam tarts from bubbling over
    while cooking, sprinkle a few drops of
    cold water onto them before cooking.

Try using tea cakes
    or hot cross buns for a tastier bread and
    butter pudding.

For an extra rich and tasty cake,
    use cold black coffee instead of milk
    in your fruit cakes.

For a moist fruit cake with extra flavour,
    grate a cooking apple into the mixture.

To make chocolate cookies
    for parties, add a ¼ cup of beer per dozen
    cookies. Or even better, some sherry...

To check the quality of baking powder,
    put a teaspoon of it in a cup of hot water.
    If the water bubbles a lot, the baking
    powder is good. If it doesn't bubble,
    throw it away.

Do your cakes crumble when cut?
After cooling and before cutting, pop them into the freezer for 20 minutes.

To improve the flavour and texture of cakes
and reduce fat at the same time, substitute a mashed banana for one third of the butter.

To make fluffier, lighter cakes,
whip the egg whites separately before adding to the recipe.

To give chocolate cakes an added kick
and to give them a rich, brown colour, add a teaspoon of instant coffee granules to each cake mix.

For a tasty, colourful cake topping
mix a little strawberry jam and boiling water into icing sugar.

It sounds obvious but the best cakes
are baked in warm kitchens. So turn on the central heating before you begin baking.

To stop cakes and pastries sticking
>to the inside of shaped cutters, brush the insides with a little oil.

To stop ice-cream melting
>in the bowl so quickly, put the bowls in the fridge for 30 minutes before serving the ice-cream.

Decorate your cakes with real flowers.
>To stop the flowers wilting, cut a 3-in/ 7.5-cm piece of a plastic drinking straw. Bend over the end of the straw and tape it securely. Fill the straw three-quarters full with water and put in the flower stem.

If you have lots of black stuff encrusted on the bottom of a baking tray,
>do not despair. Bake biscuits on the tray and they will not stick to it.

To make your sponge cakes rise,
>add a tablespoon of boiling water to the mix just before putting it in the tin.

Cakes are completely baked
>when you can stick a skewer in and it comes out clean.

Puddings

'No pudding and no fun!'
Queen Victoria

For a delicious pudding,
>add some elderberries to your apple pie.

When making custard,
>gently heat the sugar in the pan before adding the milk and your custard won't ever boil over.

To weigh golden syrup
>with minimal mess just put the whole tin on the scales and keep spooning the sticky stuff out until the tin has gone down in weight by the amount you need.

To create an impressive chocolate bowl,
> brush or pipe the smooth half of an inflated balloon with lukewarm melted chocolate until it's about ¾ in/2 cm thick. Allow to cool thoroughly, then carefully burst the balloon.

Don't waste orange or lemon peel from inside a grater
> – use a small, clean toothbrush to clean it out.

A pinch of salt added to margarine
> helps it to whisk more quickly.

Store castor sugar with rose petals,
> lemon zest or cinnamon sticks for extra flavour.

To soften hard brown sugar,
> leave it in a bowl covered with a damp tea towel overnight.

When making meringues,
you must keep the bowl completely free of grease – rub the bowl with salt and then wash it thoroughly.

To give your meringues
a toffee flavour – use brown sugar.

A quick way to mark out squares for toffee or fudge?
Lightly press a wire cooling tray onto a tin of mixture and the grid marks left behind will be a clear guide for perfect little pieces.

To light a Christmas pudding,
put brandy in a saucepan and heat gently. Place the warm brandy in a soup ladle over a lighted candle until it bursts into flames and then carefully pour this over the pudding.

Caramel sauces must not be allowed to boil.
But if yours does, don't worry – just stir in some milk or cream and turn it into toffee sauce.

If your custard goes lumpy,
> quickly put the base of the pan into some cold water and keep whisking until things are going smoothly again.

To bring out the taste of chocolate
> in most recipes, add a few coffee granules.

Avoid mess and waste
> – cut the required amounts of frozen gateaux and cakes while they're still frozen.

If sugar goes hard and lumpy
> pop it into your bread bin with a loaf and it will soon go soft.

If you have trouble slicing lemon meringue pies
> try dipping your knife into some hot water before cutting.

Left-over chocolates can be transformed

– melt them in a bowl over hot water, and add nuts and raisins. Cool the mixture, roll it into balls and chill. Delicious 'home-made' chocs!

Alternatively

spoon the hot mixture over ice-cream for an indulgent dessert.

To avoid sticky fingers

when pressing down the base for a cheese cake use a potato masher or the bottom of a mug.

Improve home-made bread and butter pudding

by adding finely grated carrot – it's a natural sweetener and adds extra texture and colour.

To make individual pavlovas,

drop the meringue mix on to the baking sheet in large dollops – they are lovely to serve at a dinner party and they also take less time to cook.

Melt your favourite chocolate bar in the microwave,
>then pour it over ice-cream for a delicious treat.

Substitute yoghurt for milk
>to make lighter scones.

For a crunchy topping
>for fruit crumbles and sweet tarts, grate some bread, then put it in a dish and bake. Mix with demerara sugar to taste and use as required.

To make pretty chocolate curls,
>microwave a choccie bar for ten seconds and then use a cheese slice to cut the curls.

If custard scrambles
>during cooking, put it in a liquidizer with a tablespoon of milk per pint of custard and spin it until it goes smooth again.

If your meringue crust cracks
> as it cools, cream spooned over it will hide it.

Keep brown sugar from going hard
> by leaving a slice of apple in the jar.

For firm meringues,
> add one teaspoon of corn-starch per dozen meringues to the sugar before beating into the egg whites.

To slice baked meringue
> easily, grease the knife with butter before cutting.

If honey is too runny
> give it a ten-second blast in microwave on the high setting. This will thicken it up slightly.

To make your mousses more decorative,
make two different mousses, one with white chocolate and one with dark. Put each in a separate, small, piping bag. Then, put both bags in one large piping bag. Squeeze into a dish, and as the mousse comes out, it will be a beautiful swirl of the two colours. The taste combination of the sweet white chocolate and the bitter dark is lovely too.

To cut cheesecake easily,
use dental floss. Hold the floss taut across the cheesecake and bring it down like a cheese slice.

To prevent ice-crystals forming on ice-cream
when stored in the freezer, stretch some cling film over the top and press the film on to the surface of the ice-cream. Put the lid on the top and pop it back into the freezer.

For a spicy version of bread and butter pudding
>use malt loaf layered with dates and bananas.

To make more meringue
>with the same number of eggs, add one tablespoon of water per egg.

To make beating brown sugar
>into a cake mix easier, put it through a food processor first – it makes it softer.

To get the best taste out of nuts in baking,
>toast them on a baking tray before adding to the mix.

To prevent mould growing on the surface of jam,
>moisten the waxed circle on top of the jar with whisky.

For really simple frozen yoghurt,
> put a lollipop stick into a carton of yoghurt, freeze and remove the carton. Try different flavours and low-fat yoghurts for a tasty slimming treat.

Try adding a layer of banana to apple pie.

Save cutting up a slab of toffee;
> pour the mixture into greased ice-cube trays for ready-made bite-sized pieces.

If you love peanuts
> and ice-cream try mixing them together for a yummy dessert.

To keep the flame burning on your Christmas pudding,
> make a little well in the top of the pudding and insert a sugar cube soaked in brandy.

If you are using baking recipes that call for liqueurs,
> rather than buy a whole bottle of one, buy a range of miniatures.

Instead of sugar,
   try golden syrup or your favourite jam in porridge.

WINE, SPIRITS AND BEER

*'They never taste who always drink;
They always talk, who never think.'*
Matthew Prior

Wine

> 'No noble man ever hated good wine.'
> François Rabelais

Pour wine
> from a height to add air and flavour.

To prevent bits of cork from getting into wine glasses,
> pour the wine through a coffee filter paper.

To serve white wine immediately
> without having to put it in an ice cooler, just store it at a temperature of 10 to 12.8°C/50 to 55.04°F.

If you haven't got a corkscrew,
> put a long screw into the top of the cork and pull it out with a piece of string.

People often say they like dry white wine best
but in blind tastings medium always
comes out top. Choose medium for the
safest bet at a dinner party.

All wines benefit from being decanted
– even if you only use a simple jug.

If champagne starts to fizz over
while you are pouring it, discreetly
dip one of your fingers into the glass!

Keep the bubbles popping.
Champagne bubbles go instantly flat
if they come into contact with detergent
so make sure your glasses are squeaky
clean. Fill the glasses to the top so that
the bubbles last as long as possible.

Store wine horizontally
to keep the corks soft.

Get your wine ready before your guests arrive
– white wine needs to be chilled for about an hour and red wine should be opened at least an hour before you intend to drink it.

If you suspect a champagne bottle
has been shaken up but you need to open it, hold it absolutely horizontal before easing the cork out.

To keep champagne really fizzy,
dangle the handle of a spoon in the top of the bottle neck.

When you're pouring champagne,
put a little in the bottom of each glass before topping them up. This stops them from overflowing and wasting all the bubbly!

It's messy when fizzy drinks overflow.
To avoid this, pour into warmed glasses and then put in lots of ice to chill.

Wine will chill much quicker with the cork out

– bear it in mind if you're in a hurry for a cool glass of wine!

Alternatively,

put the wine in an ice bucket and sprinkle salt onto the ice for a fast chill.

Don't worry if you have to decant a bottle of wine

or port at very short notice. Just pour it out very quickly to get lots of air into it.

If your decanter looks stained or dull,

fill with vinegar and crushed eggshells. Replace the stopper and give it a good hard swill round. Once rinsed with warm water, it will look as good as new.

Alternatively,

half fill the decanter with warm soapy water and two tablespoons of uncooked rice. Swish the mixture round and after half an hour remove the solution. Rinse the decanter and stand upside down to dry.

If the stopper gets stuck in a decanter,

put a few drops of cooking oil around the neck and leave it in a warm place for a while before loosening the stopper.

To separate glasses that are stuck together,

put cold water inside the inner one and place the outer one in warm water. Gently increase the temperature of the water until the outer glass expands and just lifts off. Easy!

For the true professional touch

– twist the wine bottle as you pour and avoid messy drips.

If you drink wine out of a wine box,
> remove the bag from the box when it's finished – the bag will probably contain another couple of glassfuls.

There is no actual evidence to suggest that combining the 'grape and grain' makes for worse hangovers,
> except that those who mix their drinks are probably drinking more.

Hold a bottle of chilled white wine by the neck
> rather than the body of the bottle so that your hands do not warm the wine inside.

If you're tasting wine
> always make sure your glass is tulip shaped, curving inwards towards the rim, so that when you swill the wine around it doesn't splash out all over you.

When tasting wine remember to swill it all around the mouth

as different parts of the tongue pick up different flavours.

If you really can't bear to drink very dry wine

add a spoonful of sugar to either the glass or the bottle, depending on how sweet you like it.

It is more polite to half fill your guests' glasses with wine

rather than filling them right up to the to top – they'll also get the full effect of the aromas.

Plain glasses are better for wine

as you can't see colour and clarity through cut or patterned glass.

Impress your guests with expensive wine first

– then bring out the cheaper stuff when everyone's slightly merry and they'll hardly notice the difference.

Feeling hungover?

Vitamin C is the most important ingredient in any hangover cure – the soluble flavoured vitamin tablets on the market now are virtually made for hangovers.

Most people know that red wine should be served at room temperature

but this advice comes from a time well before central heating. Room temperature means the temperature of a room with no heating – which is probably a lot colder than our heated houses. Definitely don't place your wine next to the oven or near a heater – you'll end up with something unpleasantly warm.

If you're tasting lots of wine

here's an easy way to clean your glass. After each wine pour a thimbleful of the next wine into your glass, swill it around and pour out – so you're effectively cleaning the glass with the new wine, leaving no trace of the old.

Choosing between two wines?

Taste the first, then the second, then back to the first – wines have lots of complex flavours and you'll notice subtle differences if you do this a few times – keep going until you're sure!

Magnums of wine will always be of superior quality

to the same wine in a regular-sized bottle as the ratio of wine to air is greater. So, if you can afford it or if you're entertaining go for a larger bottle.

If you find a wine you like,

look for the name of the producer rather than the name of the wine. Wines of the same name will often be made by many producers with varying degrees of quality. Better to stick to a producer you trust and try out their range of wines.

Spirits

> *'You may talk of gin and beer.'*
> Rudyard Kipling

To serve beautiful drinks

in no time, add bits of sliced fruit to an ice-cube tray and chill in the fridge beforehand. It's then easy to add as an ice substitute without all the fiddly chopping and slicing when your guests arrive.

To add that certain something to drinks,

frost the edge of the glass. Just dip the rim in some egg white followed immediately by some castor sugar. For a jazzy look, mix some food colour into the sugar.

Had a bit too much to drink?

A slice of toast with honey before you go to bed will prevent a hangover.

If you don't have a cocktail shaker,
    hold a smaller glass inverted inside
    a pint glass.

Traditionally whisky should be served
    two parts whisky to one part water –
    the water brings out the flavour.

Use mineral water instead of tap
    which can have too strong a taste and
    affect the flavour.

Ice makes whisky
    too cold and reduces its flavour.

Don't use soda in whisky
    – it ruins the taste.

Whisky evaporates
    very quickly so keep the cap tightly
    screwed on.

Whisky has a different spelling,

depending on where it comes from. Whisky is correct for Scotland, Canada and Japan: elsewhere, notably Ireland and America, it's whiskey.

The prairie oyster

is an ideal hangover cure. Rinse a glass with olive oil. Add tomato ketchup and a whole egg yolk. Season with Worcestershire sauce, vinegar, salt and pepper. Swallow the mixture in one gulp.

The best way to keep party punch cool

is to freeze some of the punch in ice-cube trays or a ring mould. Float the frozen punch in your bowl to keep it chilled but undiluted.

To decorate punch for a special occasion

core and slice apples and cut shapes for the slices using pastry cutters or a sharp knife. Dip shapes in lemon juice and float on the punch.

Treat adult party guests
>   to jelly made with a large dash of vodka.
>   Enjoy experimenting with quantities at
>   home.

For a very special party nibble,
>   inject cherry tomatoes with vodka
>   and Worcestershire sauce – sprinkle
>   with celery salt and black pepper for
>   a very original take on the traditional
>   Bloody Mary.

Flavoured vodka
>   is all the rage in pubs and clubs so try
>   making your own – cordials can be added
>   or crushed and puréed fruit. Experiment
>   with cordials that are lighter and heavier
>   than the vodka itself for a pretty layered
>   drink.

Store fresh ginger in vodka
>   – it will improve the taste of the vodka
>   and the ginger.

Beer

'He who drinks beer thinks beer.'
Washington Irving

Pouring the perfect pint is quite a skill
– beer glasses should be free from grease and rinsed in cold water just before filling. Quickly half fill the glass at an angle producing little or no foam – then slowly pour the rest of your beer into the straightened glass until a nice head forms. Cheers!

Watch where you store your bottled beer
– avoid strong light as it will really affect the taste.

Don't warm or cool beer
too quickly as the taste will suffer. This means avoiding hot water and freezers.

Store bottled beer
vertically in a cool dark place and try to drink it within six weeks – which shouldn't be too much of a problem!

Use beer to tenderize and add flavour to meat
– marinate the joint for at least one hour in your favourite tipple.

Leave open cans of beer
around the garden at barbecues and they will attract insects – thus keeping the bugs away from your guests.

When holding a garden party,
fill a child's paddling pool with ice to keep bottles cold.

Save money when throwing a party
by buying beer in small barrels or firkins. Your local landlord will advise you on what to buy and where to get it. It tastes much better too.

If you haven't got time to chill beer for your guests,
> just chill the glass instead.

SAVING THE DAY

'Accidents will occur in the best regulated families.'
David Copperfield, Charles Dickens

If your hollandaise sauce curdles,
gently stir in an ice cube.

Overcooked sauces will never improve
so don't waste your time. Some melted butter will be a delicious alternative sauce for any dish.

When making stocks or gravy,
put a chip basket inside the pan to hold bones, bay leaves and other chunky ingredients. It will make it easier to lift them all out when you have finished and saves messy sieving.

To keep the kitchen smelling sweet,
put some orange peel in the oven (at 350°F/180°C/Gas Mark 4).

Alternatively, if the pong is really strong,
boil some cloves in a mixture of one cup of water and ¼ cup of vinegar.

If you've overcooked your vegetables,
>put them in ice-cold water for a few minutes then microwave them very briefly before serving.

If disaster strikes and you burn a pan,
>leave some cold tea to soak in the pan for a few hours. The black burnt-in crust will then come away quite easily.

If you've burnt your hand,
>make up a paste of baking soda and water, and apply to the burnt area; it will really ease the pain.

If you have run out of breadcrumbs,
>use some crushed cheese biscuits instead.

Remove fruit or berry stains
>from hands with lemon juice.

To clean your microwave,
place half a lemon in a bowl of water and boil in the microwave for a few minutes. The lemony steam will vaporize all those greasy stains and say goodbye to nasty smells.

To get rid of the strong plastic smell
from new containers, wash the container then dry it and pop it in the freezer for at least two days.

To clean a food-stained pan,
fill with distilled vinegar and soak for half an hour before washing in soapy water.

To clean badly burnt saucepans,
soak in Coca-Cola for 24 hours.

If there are little bits of cork in your wine,
give the bottle a really short, sharp flick over the sink and the cork should come flying out. It's all in the wrist action!

If you still have some cork left in the bottle,
   try pouring the wine through a paper coffee filter.

Fill an ice-cube tray with left-over wine
   to use in cooking at a later date.

Breakfast cereals taste horrid when they go stale.
   Freshen things up by putting a helping in a bowl lined with kitchen towels and then heat the cereal in a microwave for 30 seconds.

This also works well for stale peanuts
   but sprinkle the paper with a little coarse salt first.

Transform slightly stale bread
   – toast and spread with a mixture of softened butter, mixed herbs and a crushed garlic clove for tasty garlic bread in seconds.

Don't throw day-old bread away,
just brush with olive oil and toast in the oven.

Don't panic if you've forgotten to heat the plates.
Just sprinkle a little hot water on each one and pop them in the microwave on 'high' for a minute or two (check that your china is microwave proof first).

Pasta should always be served on hot plates
– but if you have run out of time or space just drain the pasta over the plates to warm them.

Rejuvenate fizzy drinks
that have gone flat – add a dash of bicarbonate of soda.

If your hands smell of onions,
soak them in some milk.

If your hands are stained,
>rub the skin with a piece of raw potato. This works well on kitchen worktops too.

Prevent hangovers
>by eating a spoonful of coleslaw before going to bed. (Honest!)

Used too much chilli or curry powder?
>Save the day by adding, to a dish serving four, two tablespoons of milk.

Egg sandwiches always whiff,
>so try chopping the cooked egg and then storing it in the fridge in a covered container overnight. This should reduce the smell when you come to make up your sandwiches.

Don't get in a muddle at the supermarket checkout;
>put loose items that need weighing, like fruit and vegetables, on last to allow you time to pack your bags.

If you turn up at a restaurant
having booked a table to be told they haven't actually got one for you, the restaurant is in breach of contract and you're entitled to compensation.

And, there *is* such a thing as a free lunch...
a restaurant is actually obliged to ask you if you enjoyed your meal. If they fail to do this and you didn't really enjoy the food, you are not liable to pay the bill!

The bigger the pan you cook pasta in,
the better – the pieces won't stick together.

Rice slightly burnt and stuck to the bottom of the pan?
Don't scrape it off – it can be salvaged. Place a layer of onion skins over the rice. Leave for quarter of an hour, throw away the onion skins and serve the rice.

Do your tortillas break when you roll them?
Put them in a plastic bag and pop them in the microwave for 30 seconds and they'll be beautifully soft.

To restore the flavour to spices
that have been sitting in your cupboard for months, roast them in the oven on a high heat until you start to smell the aroma.

To clean up an egg
dropped on the floor without hassle or mess, cover the broken egg with salt and leave it for 20 minutes. It will then lift off easily and without leaving any residue.

To boil a cracked egg,
wrap it in foil, twisting the two ends into a cracker shape. Then boil as normal. When you take the foil and egg out of the water, plunge it into cold water for a moment to stop the egg cooking inside the foil.

An alternative way of boiling a cracked egg

is to put a teaspoon of salt in the water with the egg. This stops the white seeping out of the cracks.

If you've cut off the end of your hard-boiled egg

and it's still not properly cooked, place the egg (cut end up) on to a piece of cloth. Pick up the sides of the cloth and lower the egg gently into boiling water, taking care not to let any water get into the egg.

To rescue a soup or stew that's too salty,

add some raw, chopped potatoes. Remove the spuds once the dish is cooked – they will have absorbed the salt.

To prevent burnt fingers,

use ice tongs to remove tea-bags from cups.

Sloppy mashed potato?

Fold in a stiffly beaten egg white and bake in the oven.

Always throw a can of food away
> if the can has an outward bulge – the contents will be bad.

Here's a handy tip to rescue brown sugar
> that has gone hard. Put half a cup of boiling water in a microwave. Next to it put your sugar in a microwave-proof container. Put the microwave on high until the sugar has gone soft. Allow three minutes for every 1lb/450g of sugar.

If you burn your hands while handling chilli,
> rub a little vinegar over them.

To make a meal out of lettuce
> that has started to go brown, sauté it in a little olive oil with some garlic and salt.

To get rid of the smell of onions or garlic from your hands,
> rub some lemon juice on them.

To reduce excess grease
or fat in soups and stews, lay some paper towels across the surface and they will gather it.

To restore honey that has crystallized,
put it in a warm oven for a few minutes.

If your cooking oil goes black
while heating it, add a few drops of vinegar and cover with a saucepan lid. Continue heating like this for about 30 seconds and the oil should have returned to a lighter colour.

Too much garlic in a sauce or stew?
Add some parsley to neutralize it.

To absorb the smell of frying fish whilst cooking,
add celery to the pan. It tastes good too.

If you run out of eggs while baking a cake

add a teaspoon of vinegar – one teaspoon replaces one egg.

Run out of dish-washer powder?

Try baking soda.

When freezing liquid,

leave a small space at the top of the container to allow for expansion during freezing.

If all else fails...

tell your guests or family that you've decided to treat them to a surprise meal out...

INDEX

aluminium pans 151, 156
appetites, children 127
apples 51–2, 60, 79, 187, 197
  pies 178, 191, 200
  sauce 6
apricots 60
artichokes 72, 81
ashtrays 155
asparagus 71
aubergines 67, 90
avocados 67, 84

babies
  teething rings 52
  weaning 123
bacon
  alternative 29
  chopping 158
  crispy 29
  packet opening 32
  white fish fillets 45
bad breath 66, 99
Baileys Irish Cream 118
baked apples 52
baked beans 70, 77
baked potatoes 81
baking dishes 165
baking powder 160, 188
baking soda 234
baking tins 150
baking trays 159, 190
balsamic vinegar 5, 59, 91
banana trees 57
bananas 56–7, 189, 200
  bread 56
  for children 141
  hunger cravings 97
  ice-lollies 140
barbecues 54, 99, 120, 159, 170

basil 104
basting brushes 163
battering fish 43, 44
bay leaf 67, 103, 175
bean soup 5
beef 10
beer 44, 117, 218–20
bicarbonate of soda 58, 168, 227
bins 155
biscuits 117, 158, 183, 188
blood removal 26
blood sugar 134
bolognaise sauce 60
bones, fish 39, 40
bottle openers 110
bouquet garni 102
brandy 116
Brazil nuts 115
bread 3, 5, 160, 173–6, 226–7
bread and butter pudding 188, 195, 199
bread rolls 118
breadcrumbs 43, 180, 182, 224
breakfast 133
broad beans 62
broccoli 67, 73, 81
brown sauce 7
brown sugar 155, 192, 197, 199, 232
Brussels sprouts 73, 82
bubble and squeak 82
burgers 32, 167
burns 224, 232
butter
  cheddar cheese 19
  curls 168
  softening 20

cabbage 67, 75, 82, 103
cakes 183–91, 234
 decoration 150, 190
 mix 183, 199
 tins 149, 158, 184
candles 108, 111, 112, 169
capers 71
car sickness 99
car travel 136
caramel sauces 193
caraway seeds 103
cardamom 99, 112
carrots 62, 79, 195
 boiling 68
 freshness 69
 raw 76
 sex hormones 71
 tomato sauce 10
carving 27
casserole dishes 160
casseroles 4, 27, 28, 29, 109
castor sugar 192
cauliflowers 62, 68, 75, 79, 83
caviare 120
celery 31, 42, 79, 80, 233
cereals 90, 226
champagne 58, 117, 206, 207
cheddar cheese 19
cheese 19, 117
 curls 167
 freshness 18
 mould 20
 parmesan 20
 storage 18, 19, 20
 on toast 21
cheesecake 195, 198
cherries
 de-stoning 187
 glacé 185

chicken
 boneless breast 34
 left-overs 10
 plucking 26
 roasting 34
 skin removal 32
children 121–45
 baby teethers 52
 cereal 90
 milk 22
 pasta 93
chilli con carne 30
chilli peppers 68, 75, 232
chilli powder 28
 cheese on toast 21
 corn-on-the-cob 90
chilling
 beer 220
 drinks 117
 wine 117, 207, 208, 210
china, cleaning 156
chipolatas 25
chips 69
chives 103
chocolate 194, 196
 bowl 192
 cakes 189
 cookies 188
 curls 196
choking 130, 135
cholesterol 89
chop-sticks 89, 125
chopping boards 41, 151, 153, 160, 164
Christmas napkin rings 113
Christmas pudding 193, 200
chutney 9
cinnamon sticks 192
citrus fruit 53–6
cleaning

burnt food 160, 161
china 156
chopping boards 41, 151
coffee pots 160
decanters 208–9
dropped eggs 230
graters 152, 164, 192
knives 151, 152, 153
microwaves 225
ovens 151, 154, 168
pans 42, 151, 156, 157, 161, 163, 225
plates 155
 stainless steel 167
 windows 54
cleansing towels 115
cling film 157, 159, 169
cloves 178, 223
cocktail sausages 25
cocktail shakers 215
cocoa powder 10, 97
coconut, desiccated 95
cod 40
coffee 194
 cakes 188
 ice-cream 116
 instant disguise 112
 left-overs 167
 taste enhancement 113
coffee pots 160
cola
 burnt pans 225
 roasting ham 27
colds 89
coleslaw 228
consommé 115
constipation 55
contact lenses 75
corkscrews 110, 205
corn-on-the-cob 78, 83, 90
corned beef 33

cottage pie 30, 34, 157
coughing 135
Cox's apple 51
crab 38, 42–3
cranberries 57
cream
 double 19, 95
 freshness 19
 sauces 10
 whipped 19, 22
cream cheese 69
crisps 47
crumbles 196
cucumber 77
cup cakes 142
cups for children 141
curry 28
 cold cures 89
 low-fat 88
 mayonnaise 7
 sauces 9
custard 116, 118, 191, 194, 196
custard powder 184
cutlery 125, 131, 157

dairy 18–22
dates, chutney 9
dead man's fingers 43
decanters
 cleaning 208–9
 stopper stuck 209
decanting wine 206, 208
deep-fat fryers 162
digestion aid 82
digestive biscuits 113
dill seeds 103
dips 90, 116, 130
dish-washer powder 234
double cream
 alternatives 95

freshness 19
dried beans 80, 87
dried fruit 58, 96, 185
dried herbs 100, 101, 102
drinks 203–20
  at parties 120
  chilling 117
  fizzy 207, 227
  food colouring 111
  healthy 96
  non-alcoholic 111

economy 161, 162
egg-slicers 164, 167
eggs 13–18, 182, 184, 187, 234
  boiling 15, 16, 18, 230–1
  cold cures 89
  freshness 16, 21
  sandwiches 228
eggshells 208
elderberries 191
entertaining 105–20, 134
equipment 147–70
evaporated skimmed milk 95

face masks 67
farmed salmon 36
fat
  low-fat food 29
  removal 4, 29, 32, 92
filleting fish 39
filo pastry 97
firelighters 55, 93, 113
fires 113
fish 34–48, 233
  freshness 34–7
fizzy drinks 96, 227
flans 177–82
flatulence 87

flour 103, 175
flowers 115, 190
fly repellent 99
food colouring 111, 134
forks 131
frankfurters 128
freezer bags 152, 173
freezing
  chives 103
  egg whites 17
  fish 37
  flour 175
  fruit 53
  herbs 100
  left-overs 10
  lemon juice 55
  liquids 234
  meat 33
  milk 21–2
  parsley 99
  rice 94
  sweets 145
  wine 8
French toast 91
fridges 154
  food storage 114
  salad drawer 165
  smells 152–3
  tomatoes 65
frosting glasses 214
frozen foods 168
  bananas 97
  fish 36, 45
  yoghurt 200
fruit 49–61, 93, 129
  see also individual fruits
  cakes 185, 188
  for children 143
  crumble 95
  juice 30, 141, 145
  pies 180, 181

pizzas 182
stains 224
storage 60, 165
fruit salad 54, 57, 58
fudge 193

gammon 26, 28
garlic 233
　bad breath 99
　chopping 69
　frying 102
　peeling 65, 74
　planting 71
　popcorn 102
　smell 232
　storage 64, 81
　subtle flavour 80, 81
garlic bread 175
germs 156
ginger 30, 99, 101, 217
ginger biscuits 117
ginger bread 97
glasses 110, 211
　frosting 214
　separating 209
Golden Delicious 51
golden syrup 191, 201
gooseberries 57
granita 98
grapefruit juice 96
grapefruits 54
grapes 60, 66
graters 152, 164, 192
grating 54, 163
gravy 7, 11, 223
　fat removal 32
　granules disguise 108
　low-fat 29
　stock making 6
　thickening 9
　tomato juice 64

grease removal 5, 31, 233
green peppers 81, 116
grilling fish 46

haddock 47
hake 42
ham
　dried out 26
　roasting 27
hangovers 210, 212, 214, 216, 228
hard boiled eggs 15, 16, 17
haricot beans 70
healthy options 85–104
heating 119
herbs 9, 98–104, 110
hollandaise sauce 223
honey 158, 174, 197, 214, 233
　pork marinade 30
　sandwich filling 11
honeydew melon 58
horse-radish 83
hygiene 139

ice 114, 215
　children's soup 125
　coffee pot cleaning 160
　fat removal 4, 29, 92
　whisky 215
ice-cream 19, 116, 190, 195, 196, 198, 200
ice-lollies 140–1, 142
iced tea 119
icing 150, 167, 187, 189
icing sugar 186
indigestion 99
insects 141

jag 127
jam 189

mould 199
porridge 201
tarts 188
jar lids 152
jelly 166, 217

kebab skewers 162
ketchup 163
kitchen scales 159
kiwi fruit 30
kiwis 164
knives
 cheese cutting 117
 cleaning 151, 152, 153
 cutting raisins 165
 perfect slicing 154
 rust-free 152, 153
 safety 167
 sharpening 151

lasagne 157
lemon juice
 apple browning 52
 cauliflowers 83
 cleaning microwaves 225
 extraction 53, 55
 few drops 56
 fish smells 41, 42
 freezing 55
 fridge smells 153
 fruit browning 60
 gammon 26
 herbs 102
 meat curry 28
 mushroom soup 5
 quiche 180
 rice 79
 rice whitening 95
 salad dressing 9
 smell removal 232
 stain removal 224

 tough meat 27
lemon meringue pies 194
lemon peel 52, 54, 192
lemon rind 30, 55
lemon zest 192
lemonade 58, 115
lemons 53–4, 155, 160
lentils 71, 87
lettuce 31, 63, 65, 78, 232
lighting 89, 115
lime 30, 90
liqueurs 200
liquorice root 99
lobster 38, 43

magnums 213
margarine 192
marinating 11, 27, 30, 186, 219
marmite 11
marshmallows 120, 142
mashed potato 4, 9, 69, 83, 91, 181, 231
mayonnaise 7, 11, 20
meat 23–34
 cooking for children 128, 129
 marinating 11
 pre-cooking 109
 tenderizing 219
medication 96
melon 58
meringue 193, 197, 199
mice 175
microwaves 154, 162
 brown sugar 232
 chocolate 196
 cleaning 225
 cleansing towels 115
 trout 47
milk 26, 142–3, 145, 227

boiling 153
freezing 21–2
haddock 47
storage 21
milk shakes 19, 56
mincemeat 181
mineral water 113
mint 99, 103
mint jelly 68
mites 175
mixing bowls 161
monkfish 40
mould
 cheese 20
 fruit 52
 jam 199
moulds 166
mousses 198
muesli 19
mushrooms 62
 frying 87
 soup 5
 storage 66
 water saving 5
music 119
mussels 37–8
mustard 113
 fish smells 41
 flavouring 9
 gravy 11

naan 174
napkin rings 113, 170
nuts 61, 95, 115, 199

oils 161, 233
 flavouring 9
 olive oil 33, 71, 74, 79, 181, 184
olives 84
omelettes 15, 16, 18

onions 229
 burnt pans 156
 chopping 72
 finely chopped 63
 frying 63, 102
 peeling 78
 salads 63
 smell 63, 74, 227, 232
 soup colour 3
 storage 64, 80, 82
 tears prevention 64, 66, 74
oranges 53, 54–5
 juice 55
 peel 52, 54, 55, 192, 223
 rind 55
ovens
 cleaning 151, 154, 168
 racks 164
 space 109

pans
 burnt 156, 224, 225
 cleaning 42, 151, 156, 157, 161, 163, 225
 copper-bottomed 160, 162, 163
 covering 158
 storage 163
paprika 9
parmesan cheese 20
parsley 62, 98–9, 101, 233
pasta 93, 227, 229
pasta bake 94
pastry 88, 97, 177–8, 179, 180
pastry cutters 149
pavlovas 195
peanut butter 71
peanuts 200, 226
pesto 179
pheasant 26

picnics 118, 141
pies 90, 177–82
pineapples 59, 61
piping bags 150, 163, 165
pitta bread 174
pizza 125, 149, 160, 181–2
plaice 36, 39
plane travel 137
plates
  cleaning 155
  fish smells 42
  size 89
  warming 120, 227
poached eggs 17
popcorn 102
pork
  crackling 25
  marinade 30
  scoring 25
porridge 19, 201
porridge oats 3
port 5, 208
portions 126, 128
potato peelers 167
potatoes
  baked 81
  boiling 75, 80
  croquettes 70
  discolouring 64
  mashed 4, 9, 69, 83, 91, 181, 231
  mint jelly 68
  roast 87
  roasting 68, 82
  salty casseroles 28
  salty soups 231
  size 82
  soup thickening 3
  sprouting prevention 77
  stain removal 228
  storage 80

vinegar 91
water saving 4
poultry 32
Prairie Oyster 216
presentation 110
prune juice 3
puddings 96, 191–201
puff pastry 179
pumpkin 97
punch 216
Puy lentils 87

quails' eggs 17
quiche 179–80

raisins 60, 165
ray 37
red cabbage 76
red peppers 66, 73, 116
red wine 10, 207, 212
restaurants 137–8, 229
rhubarb 58, 96, 156, 158
rice 110, 114, 155, 159, 209, 229
  freezing 94
  moulds 94
  sticking prevention 79
  stirring 70
  whitening 95
roasting
  chicken 33
  ham 27
  potatoes 68, 82, 87
  poultry 32
  spices 100
  turkey 31
roasting tins 157
roe 36
rolling pins 149, 180
rose petals 73, 107, 192
royal icing 150

safety, knives 167
sage 104
salad cream 70
salad dressing 7, 9, 70
salads
  freshness 67
  onions 63
salmon 36, 39–40
salt 166, 192, 231
  casseroles 28
  cellars 155
  coffee pot cleaning 160
  corn-on-the-cob 78
  fish 47
  fruit pies 181
  pan cleaning 160
  pork crackling 25
  reduction 103
  sauces 8
  vegetables 76
sandwich filling 11
sandwich spread 79
sandwiches 118, 126, 228
sardine tins 48
sauces 6–11
  bolognaise 60
  caramel 193
  chilli 68
  hollandaise 223
  overcooked 223
  too garlicky 233
sausages 25, 29
scales 159
scones 183, 196
scotch eggs 182
scrambled eggs 16, 18, 20, 158
scrapbooks 159
sesame seeds 61
shallots 75
shallow-frying fish 43

shark 37
shepherd's pie 30, 69
sherry 5
shopping lists 168, 169
shortbread 183, 184
sieving 152, 186
sifting 166
skate 37
skinning fish 39, 46
slicing 154
  meat 27
  meringue 197
  tuna 47
smells 223
  bins 155
  broccoli 73, 81
  cabbage 67, 75, 103
  cauliflower 75
  egg sandwiches 228
  fish 41, 42, 233
  fridges 152–3
  garlic 232
  microwaves 225
  onions 63, 74, 227, 232
  plastic 225
smoked fish 36, 37
smoking 99
snacks 126–7
soda water 16, 114, 215
soft drinks 111
soups 1–5
  cauliflower leaves 79
  for children 125
  consommé 115
  fat removal 92
  garlic 80
  going further 108
  thickening 3, 4, 91
  tinned 92
  too salty 231
  vegetable 88

spaghetti 92, 93
spices 9, 98–104, 230
spirits 214–17
sponge cakes 184, 185, 190
spoons 131
spring onions 21
stainless steel 167
stains 26, 224, 228
steaming fish 46
stews 32
stinging nettles 72
stir-fry 73
stock 4, 68, 223
  cubes 100, 101
  grease removal 31
  left over gravy 6
  water 11
storage
  apples 52, 79
  beer 218, 219
  biscuits 158
  carrots 69, 79
  castor sugar 192
  celery 79
  cheese 18, 19, 20
  eggs 16
  flour 103, 175
  food in fridges 114
  fruit 60, 165
  garlic 64, 81
  herbs 100, 101
  lemons 53
  lettuce 78
  lobster 38
  milk 21
  mushrooms 66
  onions 64, 80, 82
  pans 163
  potatoes 80
  strawberries 60
  tomatoes 65, 80

vegetables 60, 165
vol-au-vents 179
wine 206
storage bags 165
strawberries 59, 60
string beans 76
stuffing 31, 182
stuffing mix 101
sugar 155, 192, 194
  cheese boxes 18
  fish battering 44
  lettuce 65
  mashed potato 69
  onion frying 63
  pies 178
sweets 144–5
syrup 158

tablecloths
  candlewax 111, 112
  stain disguise 107
tables, protection 107
tasting
  food 166
  wine 210–11, 212–13
tea, iced 119
tea ball 103
tea cakes 188
tea-bags 231
teapots 155
teething rings 52
tenderizing meat 28, 30, 32, 33, 219
thickening
  gravy 9
  sauces 10
  soups 3, 4, 91
tinned food 169, 232
  beans 87
  soups 5, 92
  tomatoes 64

vegetables 83
toasters 168
toffee 193, 200
tomatoes 156
  banana ripening 56
  ketchup 163
  ripening 65
  sauce 10
  skinning 73
  soggy 64
  storage 65, 80
  tinned 64
tongue 26
tooth decay 96, 127, 144
tortillas 230
trout 35, 40, 47
tuna 47
turkey
  flavour 31
  free-range 33
  fruit juice 30
  left-overs 31
  minced 92
  rashers 29
  roasting 31
  stop sticking 31
turnips 67

vegetable broth 73
vegetables 62–84, 93
  see also individual
    vegetables
  boiling in advance 117
  car travel 136
  for children 129–30
  left-overs 10, 78
  overcooked 224
  soup 5, 88
  storage 60, 165
  water saving 7
vegetarians 109

vinegar 5, 164
  cakes 234
  candles 112
  carrots 76
  cauliflowers 83
  cheese freshness 18
  chutney 9
  cleaning decanters 208
  cleaning pans 156, 225
  cleaning plates 155
  fish smells 42
  flavouring 9
  kitchen smells 223
  oil blackening 233
  poached eggs 17
  pork crackling 25
  potatoes 75, 91
  red cabbage 76
  strawberries 59
  tenderizing meat 28, 33
vodka 217
vol-au-vents 179

water
  boiling quickly 114
  freshness 66
watercress 66
watermelons 59
weight loss 88, 90
Welsh rarebit 100
whipped cream 19, 22
whipping eggs 16
whisky 215–16
white fish fillets 36, 45
white sauce 6
white wine 205, 206, 207, 210
window cleaning 54
wine 92, 203–13
  boxes 210
  chilling 117, 207, 208, 210

cork debris 205, 225–6
freezing 8
left-over 10
sauces 8
woks 154, 158

yeast 173
yellow peppers 81
yoghurt 20, 96, 196, 200
  low-fat 97
  milk shake 19
  salad dressing 9
  soups 4